LAST OF HIS KIND

An Informal Portrait of Harry S. Truman

By

CHARLES ROBBINS

WITH PHOTOGRAPHS AND CAPTIONS BY

BRADLEY SMITH

WILLIAM MORROW AND COMPANY, INC.
NEW YORK 1979

LAST OF HIS KIND

An Informal Portrait of Harry S. Truman

Copyright © 1979 by William Morrow and Company, Inc.

Grateful acknowledgment is made to Faber and Faber, Ltd., and Harcourt Brace Jovanovich, Inc., for permission to quote from THE WASTE LAND by T. S. Eliot.

Library of Congress Cataloging in Publication Data

Robbins, Charles.
    Last of his kind.

    Includes index.
    1. Truman, Harry S., Pres. U.S., 1884-1972. 2. Presi-dents—United States—Biography. I. Smith, Bradley.
II. Title.
E814.R6   973.918′092′4 [B]   79-1201
ISBN 0-688-03447-0

BOOK DESIGN   CARL WEISS

Printed in the United States of America.

First Edition

1 2 3 4 5 6 7 8 9 10

Contents

XI

INDEPENDENCE AGAIN

XII

RETROSPECTIVE

Author's Note

As they went their underpaid rounds, reporters in the old days used to encourage each other with the saying, "You meet such interesting people"; it was one of the consolations of journalism.

I was often reminded of the words while collecting the material for this book. In fact, the book has become for me less a thing in itself than a kind of keepsake of the interesting and generous people who helped so much with it. To cite them all would be to tempt the reader to skip them all, so I am confining this official salute to the comparative few without whom there would have been no book.

My thanks go first to Dr. Benedict K. Zobrist, Director of the Harry S. Truman Library in Independence, Missouri, and his splendid staff, especially Philip D. Lagerquist and Elizabeth Safly; then to Lawrence A. Yates, a researcher impressively versed in the library's contents (he introduced me to the Truman autobiographical sketch, which proved to be indispensable, as well as luckily in the public domain); to Ernest V. Heyn, who first brought me together with Truman, Thomas J. Fleming, historian and novelist, who encouraged me to return to Independence, and John C. Willey, editor, who made it possible for me to make the trip. Colonel Rufus Burrus, Mr. and Mrs. Andrew Gray and former Secretary of the Treasury John W. Snyder all selflessly lent me their ears and reminiscences, as did Mary Jane Truman, Fred Truman and Frances Myers. And finally and profoundly I wish to thank former Secretary of State Dean Acheson's son, David, who made available to me the excerpts of his father's papers, which give this volume its most stimulating pages.

Since I have been reading books, magazine articles and newspaper stories about Harry Truman from the time of our first meeting in 1953 until the present, it would be next to impossible to list them all, as well as inappropriate in a work of this informal character. However, passing over the two latter categories entirely, I should like to mention a few books which have broadened my knowledge of Truman and in that way contributed indirectly to the portrait of him in these pages. They are:

Memoirs, by Harry S. Truman, 2 vols., Garden City, New York, 1955–1956.

Mr. Citizen, by Harry S. Truman, New York, 1953.

Truman Speaks, by Harry S. Truman, New York, 1960.

Mr. President, by William Hillman, New York, 1952.

Souvenir, by Margaret Truman, New York, 1956.

Harry S. Truman, by Margaret Truman, New York, 1973.

The Man of Independence, by Jonathan Daniels, New York, 1971.

The Man from Missouri, by Alfred Steinberg, New York, 1962.

Harry Truman and the Crisis Presidency, by Bert Cochran, New York, 1973.

Plain Speaking: An Oral Biography of Harry S. Truman, by Merle Miller, New York, 1974.

Conflict and Crisis: The Presidency of Harry S. Truman, 1945–1948, by Robert J. Donovan, New York, 1977.

The Pendergast Machine, by Lyle W. Dorsett, New York, 1968.

Documents in the archives of the Harry S. Truman Library, in Independence, Missouri, supplied the quotations from the following persons: Harry H. Vaughan, Edward D. McKim, Frederick J. Bowman, Henry Chiles, Ethel Noland, Mrs. W. L. C. Palmer, Mathew J. Connelly, Mize Peters, Gaylon Babcock, Ted Marks, Stanley Woodward, Mildred Dryden, Harry Easeley, Charles F. Curry, Eben Ayers and H. V. Kaltenborn.

CHARLES ROBBINS

Schodack Landing, New York
July 15, 1978

Photographer's Note

MY MEETING WITH HARRY TRUMAN IN THE SUMMER OF 1953, AND THESE candid photographs of him, were the direct result of my photographing Helen Keller a year earlier and Mahatma Gandhi seven years earlier. When *The American Weekly* decided to run a series of illustrated articles called "Mr. Citizen" written by Harry S. Truman, describing what life was like for a former President, the editors considered various photographers' portfolios and dispatched their choices to the former President in Independence, Missouri. He liked the Keller and Gandhi pictures and I got the assignment. I packed my cameras and was on my way to Independence, Kansas City and, later, Washington, D.C.

In Independence I found that getting up before dawn to meet Citizen Truman for his morning walk was no problem. It had been necessary when photographing Gandhi to walk with him at 5 A.M.—which meant getting up at four. Helen Keller was also an early riser. Blind Miss Keller could not see the sunrise but she liked to sit in her picture window facing east so that she could feel the warmth of the sun as it came over the horizon. Again it was necessary for me to be up and about by 4 A.M. By the time I got the Truman assignment I was beginning to feel that I would be typed as a predawn photographer.

Of these three world figures Harry Truman proved to be by far the most difficult to keep ahead of—and if a photographer cannot keep ahead of his subject, there are no pictures. So I would arrange for an early-morning taxi, get five or six hours of sleep and arrive at the Truman home between 5 and 5:30 A.M.

There were always people waiting for the former President to appear. One morning Truman, looking out a window, saw me waiting and clicked the gate lock open from inside the house—so that I could have a look at the front yard and decide on the best place to photograph him when he came out to pick up the paper. While I moved about, mentally composing pictures, a pair of tourists—husband and wife—drove up. They were too impatient to wait for the appearance of the President and decided a snapshot of the house would do, but they did want a figure in the picture. "Do you work here?" asked the man. I said, "Yes—I guess so." "Well," he said, "would you mind picking a flower or two off that bush so I can get some life into the picture?"—and I became a part of his Truman picture collection.

Once the walk started, Truman moved more like a slow jogger than a fast walker. I spent a good part of the hour-and-a-half walk running ahead of him, stopping briefly to take a picture from across the street or from the street corner. He managed to ignore my presence, which was probably easy for him after being surrounded constantly by Secret Service security men in Washington.

We dropped in at an early-morning café across from the police station. Truman knew the officers sitting there, and the proprietor. I was starving after my mile-and-a-quarter run and the ex-President suggested that I try the buckwheat cakes while he had a cup of coffee. The cakes were so good that I was sure they must have been made from some special stone-ground wheat. When Truman asked the proprietor for the recipe, he replied, "Aunt Jemima." The policemen laughed us out of the café.

I've tried to report on our travels and adventures in the captions given with the selection of pictures that follows, taken from the hundreds of photographs I made. What did I think of my subject? My most lasting impression of Harry S. Truman was of a kind, thoughtful man who was determined to have time for everyone. He was even thoughtful enough to write letters to my wife and six children apologizing for keeping me in Kansas City over my birthday—and he appended handwritten notes to each of them. Later Truman sent back one of the pictures I had taken of him on the screened porch. On it he had written, "To a great photographer —from one who knows—Harry Truman, 1953."

For those who may someday photograph a President or former President, here are the technical notes: cameras—Rolleiflex (2¼ x 2¼), Pentax (35 mm.), Deardorff (8 x 10); film—Monochrome Plus X, Color Kodachrome; lighting—available light only. Year—1953.

BRADLEY SMITH

La Jolla, California
September 6, 1978

I

Independence, 1953

IT WAS HOT THAT SPRING, 103°, 104°, DAY AFTER DAY. MY TWO JOURnalist colleagues and I had something that passed for air conditioning in our hotel, but it was conspicuously absent from the Truman home in Independence. The lack didn't seem to bother the former President and his wife. Taking the weather as it came, he told us, was better than monkeying with it. As we sat with him and Mrs. Truman in their old-fashioned living room, we talked about that and the state of the world and the articles we were working on. The conversation was so easygoing that sometimes I'd forget to take notes. Then a reference of his to Churchill or Stalin or de Gaulle would remind me that this was History, and, feeling a little chilled, despite the heat, I'd start scribbling again.

All that happened long ago, but memory keeps bringing it back. An overheard phrase can conjure it up or a glimpse of a face in the street or of a hat, worn just so. Lately the conjuror has been an ambiguous feature of our society that every year is affecting the lives of more and more Americans—retirement.

Like the river, which comedian Jimmy Savo used to plead with to stay away from his door, retirement started lapping a while ago at the doors of a number of friends and then at mine. Dive in and enjoy it, the ads say, but I put off doing so as long as possible. When at last I had to take the plunge, I fortified myself with every available remedy, the most helpful of which was the remembrance of the weeks I spent in Independence in 1953, the first year of Truman's retirement.

Only a few months earlier he had been President of the United States, and now here he was, at sixty-nine, a private citizen again, retired. I recall his commenting on the number of people who kept seeking him out on the chance that he might be able to help them find employment.

"They seem to forget that I'm one of the unemployed myself."

If the pain of retirement is proportionate to the value of the job one has left, he should have been suffering the maximum. Somehow, though, he had managed to take the change in stride, even to find satisfaction in it. His attitude impressed me at the time. Today it seems extraordinary. In fact, I've come to think of it as not just a particular attitude in the face of a special situation but the expression of a deeply American way of life. As such, it may be worth some study, especially now when there are so many different ideas of what the word "American" means.

The only thing even approaching a complaint I ever heard him offer was the opinion that former Presidents and Vice-Presidents should be made ex officio members of the Senate:

"That way they could give the country the benefit of their experience without stepping on anybody's political toes," he said and added, "At the moment, of course, it isn't much of a problem, because there are only two of us, Hoover and me. Back in 1861 there were five, Van Buren, Tyler, Fillmore, Pierce and Buchanan. So far as I know that was the only time anybody ever considered making use of them. It was hoped they might be able to figure out a way of staving off the war—the Civil War. There were plans for them to get together and talk it over, with Van Buren presiding, but he had second thoughts and nothing came of it."

Truman's transition to private life was the subject of the articles we were preparing. He was already under contract to write his memoirs for *Life* magazine, with publication also in *The New York Times* and *St. Louis Post-Dispatch* and with Doubleday bringing them out in book form. But Ernest V. Heyn, editor of *The American Weekly* (I was then on the staff of this Sunday supplement of the Hearst and other newspapers), had interested his literary aide, William Hillman, in having him write a preliminary series for us.

The suggested title, *Mr. Citizen*, had something to do with winning Hillman's favor, since it was a bow toward his own best-selling book, *Mr. President*. Truman, for his part, liked the idea of being paid and publicized by his old detractor, Hearst. For as he once said to me, "There is no praise sweeter than the praise of former enemies."

At any rate, the *American Weekly* articles would be his first writing since leaving office and, as such, seemed to represent a scoop of sorts.

Heyn, who was stationed in New York, made me the field director of the project, a rather risky move, since my knowledge of the subject was slight. Such preconceptions as I had of the thirty-third President had been diminished by my admiration for the thirty-second, as well as by the fact that the only times I had seen or heard him had been while he was making speeches, an exercise at which he did not shine.

My mental picture of him was that of a Babbitty type who onstage was rigid and prosaic, offstage prone to unfortunate lapses into folksiness. Hillman added a few touches to this caricature. A former International News Service correspondent turned radio newscaster, he viewed himself as a behind-the-scenes manipulator, a Richelieu, dealing in matters of international importance. No one about to be presented at court could have been subjected to instructions more elaborate than those he gave me before our departure for Kansas City: they covered everything from how to address the former President to what subjects to avoid.

Afterward, I wondered if he might have been having a little fun at my expense; his sense of humor tended to be devious. If so, he succeeded, for I was wholly unprepared for the warmth and naturalness Truman showed when we met for the first time at a luncheon in one of the Hotel Muehlebach's private dining rooms. Still, I did not at once surrender my caricature of him. An incident that occurred at the start of the meal helped me hold on to it.

Heyn, who had come to Kansas City for the introductory ceremonies, arrived in the dining room with a telegram from our New York office announcing that the Eisenhower administration had just fired George Kennan, head of the State Department's Policy Planning Staff. When shown the message, Truman remarked, "That's too bad." Then, after reading further, he came to a point where Kennan was referred to as having "formulated Truman's policy of containment."

"The son of a bitch should have been fired," he said, making it clear, however, that he was condemning not Kennan but only this inexact reference to him by adding amiably, "I always liked him, even though I couldn't figure out what he was talking about half the time."

The performance seemed to support the caricature—at least the folksy, one-of-the-boys part of it.

After Heyn and Hillman had flown back to New York, Bradley Smith, the free-lance photographer we had engaged for this series, Warren Hall, of our staff, and I settled down to work. While Smith went around taking the stunning photographs that appear in these pages (only a few were published with the *American Weekly* articles), Hall and I began interviewing the former President and his family and friends. I had brought with me one of the cumbersome tape recorders of those days, but Truman seemed ill at ease with it, so I took my notes in pencil and decanted them into the recorder at night.

One thing was obvious from the start: he had studied the business of retirement, thought it through in advance, as he liked to do with every problem. A number of high-salaried jobs had been offered him (in some he'd have had to do little more than draw his pay) and, although he was far from wealthy, he had turned them down for fear that in one way or another they would detract from the dignity of his former office.

The rest of his life, he had decided, was going to be spent paying the country back for the favors it had done him. Central to his plan was the Truman Library, which was then in the blueprint stage and which, with its invaluable papers and White House souvenirs, was later given to the United States. Seeing this project through to completion, writing, teaching and accommodating the people who still were coming to him for aid and advice kept him busy. Indeed, his secretary, Rose Conway, said that her work load in Missouri was about the same as it had been in Washington.

A native of Kansas City, she had returned home on the train with the Trumans, and her parting words with him had been brief and typical:

"Good night."

"See you at the office," he said.

"Tomorrow?"

"Day after. We'll have to unpack tomorrow."

"Usual time?"

"Yes."

So, after a day off for unpacking, it was business as usual for both of them.

But the fact that it had a purpose was not the only favorable aspect of his retirement. Even more important was the setting. Instead of following the trend of pulling up stakes and going someplace warmer, cheaper, more glamorous or whatnot, he went home. And, as one whose parents had uprooted themselves from the Midwest and been Easternized, I was interested in what home meant to him and Mrs. Truman.

In her view, the time spent in Washington had been a kind of exile. When it was over and she and her husband arrived back in Independence, with cheering crowds at the station and on their street, she observed that this welcome almost made up for the years of trouble they had been through. Settled again in the house her grandfather had built, surrounded by order and security (not the Secret Service kind), she was content.

In Truman's own case, the most sustaining thing about home seemed to be the evidence there of the past. Some people, including many of the retired, try to use the past as an escape from the present. He used it to put the present in perspective: it gave him a handy frame of reference.

My pleasantest recollections of that time are those of sharing his early morning walks or sitting beside him as he drove to some neighboring scene of interest. Independence on the threshold of a new day was as exhilarating as any place could be at such an hour. The trees shading the quiet streets looked buoyant, as though about to rise and lift the town gently out of sleep. The houses, with their wide verandahs, gables and cupolas, were quaint and friendly. The whole place was like a Midwestern Grover's Corners miraculously preserved in its turn-of-the-century freshness and innocence. You would not have been surprised to see Tom Sawyer or Penrod come whistling around the corner.

A block from the Truman home was the site of his old high school. The original building, along with its records, had been destroyed by fire, but, he liked to say, anybody who doubted he'd gone to school could inquire of one of his surviving teachers, Mrs. W. L. C. Palmer, a spry old lady with undimmed memories of him as a student. Still standing nearby was the church in whose Sunday school he told me he had first met Bess—"the prettiest girl I'd ever seen—and she still is. . . ."

Then we would come to the home of a Mr. Mercer, who, as Treasurer of Missouri, Truman said, "had made himself rich by lending out state money and putting the interest in his pocket.

"My grandfather introduced me to him when I was a boy. Old Mercer was running for county judge then, and my grandfather suggested that if the people of the state ever found out what he'd done with their money he might have a hard time getting elected. But the old man just smiled and said he was sure nobody could prove anything against him."

We would pass the courthouse, which Truman had had rebuilt when *he* was county judge and still viewed with pride, then the Mormon Temple, holy of holies of the Church of Jesus Christ of Latter-day Saints. The Mormons had split into two groups in Independence, he told me, with Brigham Young leading one of them farther west, while Joseph Smith and his brother took the other back to Illinois—and to their own lynching. And he mentioned the Oregon and Santa Fe Trails, which started here, and Jesse James, a local legend, and the long, still bitterly remembered War Between the States.

On days when we drove he would point out other marks of his years as county judge, in particular the network of roads he had given the taxpayers. He had modeled these roads on ones he had seen in France in World War I, and they still were well preserved. Finally we'd arrive at the town of Grandview and on its outskirts the Truman farm, which he had worked for a dozen years before going off to the war and which now was being run by his younger brother, Vivian.

Having so far failed to find a place for his library in Independence, he was thinking of putting it on forty or sixty acres of the farm, which he would present to the government—no mean gift from a man of his means.

"And I might build myself a new old-fashioned house to go with it. I've never had a house of my own." But after a moment he added, "I don't want to be secluded, though. It's being with people that makes you happy —helping people."

His leisurely travelogues made up a short course in the history of the area, delivered not nostalgically or pedagogically but with a dry matter-of-factness reminiscent of Mark Twain or Will Rogers (two of his favorite characters). "I was President of the country," he seemed to be saying "but I don't want to forget I'm also the fellow who went to that school and plowed a pretty straight furrow on this farm."

An anecdote of his made the same point; it was about his mother. On being asked if she was proud to have a son in the White House, she had replied, yes, but she was just as proud of her other son in the farmhouse down the road.

And then he'd say that he didn't want to be buried in Arlington Cemetery but right around here, because "a man should be buried where his home is, where he belongs." And he'd add with a grin that a memorial would not be necessary, because "I'll be cussed and discussed for the next generation anyway."

Still, it might be asked, is it such a good thing to be reminded always of the past, especially in a country where the accent is so heavily on youth? After being eased out of whatever one's been doing, isn't it better to forget the past and find a place where the illusion of being young again can be enjoyed for a while?

A friend of mine thought so. Before moving to the retirement haven he had carefully selected, he told me how great everything was going to be: fishing, swimming, golf, etc. That was three years ago. Now he's bored. Worse still, he's disoriented. Appearances to the contrary notwithstanding, teenagers are not alone in suffering identity crises. You can also have one late in life. My friend knew well enough who he had been yesterday, but who was he today? There was nothing in sight to help him get his bearings. Living in an anonymous house in an anonymous community, he was becoming anonymous himself.

In Independence, Truman was neither bored nor disoriented. As a young man he had had thirty-nine cousins, he told me ("I was the only one in the family they all spoke to; it was my first experience in diplomacy."); Mrs. Truman had had about the same number, and a good percentage of both lots was around in 1953. Even more numerous were their friends. The men he often had lunch with at the Hotel Muehle-bach made up the inner circle; they reflected the various phases of his life: the World War I period, on whose associations his whole career had been founded, his postwar fling at business (personified by his former partner, Eddie Jacobson), and the local political base camps from which he had made the long climb to the White House.

Visible everywhere in people and places, the past was always giving him his bearings.

As I slowly got to know him, my estimate of Truman underwent a couple of revisions. There was the initial surprise of finding him so companionable. Next, after hearing him say more or less the same things to others he'd been saying to me, I began to think he was playing the part of the neighborly ex-President. But then this thought was supplanted by another, which with some modifications has remained with me: namely, that he did have a sort of act but that it was one any intelligent person in his place would have resorted to. As a public character, he was bombarded with the same questions and effusions over and over; if he had tried to reply differently on each occasion, he would have had time for little else. Instead of spoiling him, the act helped to keep him unspoiled.

His relationship with his close friends, the Muehlebach circle, contributed to this last view. With them there were no false notes on either side. Without surrendering his dignity, he managed in their company to be a friend but also to remain a little apart, his own man. And I wondered if something of this same sort might have marked—and to some extent might explain—his peculiar relationship with boss Tom Pendergast and the Pendergast political machine. Truman had often been criticized for that connection, but even his most dedicated foes had had to admit that somehow he had escaped contamination.

His relationship with his wife also impressed me. Her public image (of a rather dowdy housewife) was as far from the reality as the image of him I had brought to Independence. She was full of charm, with a repressed girlish mischievousness and a dry wit that quickly let the air out of pretense and righted departures from common sense. Even when he was their target, as frequently happened, her comments entertained him. After thirty-four years of marriage, they obviously still enjoyed each other's company.

In her presence, I once asked him if he held to his spartan early morning schedule every day. "Most of the time," he answered, while she made a sound which in the dialogue of yesterday's novels was rendered as "humph!"

Another morning, when he got back to the house, she said, as he had predicted she would, that she didn't see why he couldn't be out pushing the lawn mower instead of taking a walk. He replied that he couldn't push it on Sunday, she wouldn't let him and people wouldn't think well of him if he did. But, he went on, he'd be happy to mow the lawn, if she'd let him get one of those mowers you could ride around on.

This little ritual evidently pleased them both.

Late in June we concluded our coverage of the Trumans by following them to Washington on their first trip back since leaving the White House. They went alone in their car, and he did the driving in his usual fast time of two and a half days. He had a Library Committee meeting to attend in the capital and also a speech to give to the Reserve Officers in Philadelphia. They arrived on a Sunday afternoon. Bradley Smith joined them that day at the Mayflower Hotel, I, the following morning.

Their daughter, Margaret, who then was pursuing her singing career in New York City, had come to Washington for this occasion; it was my first sight of her. She had got in the day before and was flying around as a kind of press secretary, obviously enjoying the role. A full-scale press conference, which she had arranged, was going on when I came in.

The chance to see the Trumans all together in their second home, Washington, bridged gaps in my knowledge of them. He was like a kid on a holiday, exchanging quips with the newsmen, welcoming his former staff and members of his cabinet, hurrying from one telephone to another to talk to senators, representatives, judges. "The Democratic faithful," as one local newspaper put it, "beat a path to the Mayflower." All in the shadow of a White House which throughout his four-day stay maintained a tomblike silence—he had a quip for this, too. When a reporter asked if he were going to see Ike, he said:

"He hasn't time to see every Tom, Dick and Harry that comes to town."

He had told me a little about his relationship with the man who had succeeded him. It had soured during the campaign when Republican senators Joseph McCarthy and William Jenner had demagogically charged General George Marshall with treason. Truman, who idolized Marshall, had damned them for it and gone on publicly to damn Eisenhower for letting them get away with it. But, as usual after a campaign, he had been willing to let bygones be bygones. Eisenhower, less used to the ways of politics, had continued to nurse his resentment, as he'd made clear by snubbing Truman on Inauguration Day—and now he was doing it again.

After the morning press conference, Smith and I were invited to a staff meeting at which the final touches were to be put on the speech to the Reserve Officers, the former President's first major address since returning to private life. Truman had outlined what he wanted to say before leaving home and there had been some discussion of it, I gathered, by telephone and letter. His staff had then worked up a first draft, which he was seeing today for the first time.

It was a lively exegetical session. He would read a line or two aloud, then pause for comment. From the ensuing argument, the laughter and byplay, there slowly emerged a different speech. "I wouldn't say it that way," he would remark. "How about this—" And out would go a few two-dollar words to be replaced by twenty-five-cent ones. The final product was pretty much all his. But it was plain where his speechmaking trouble lay: each time he read aloud from the script he was flat; when he just talked, especially with animation, he was on key, or what is accepted as key in his hometown.

"Lunch with Missouri congressional delegation at Capitol," my notes of the day continue. "Speaker's dining room (?). Reps. Cannon and Rayburn hosts. Truman-Rayburn like long-separated brothers. Sat across from them next to Symington, who seemed to feel a little out of it. Truman sure the Dems. were on the comeback trail. 'We gave them three-hundred-dollar cows, now they've got thirty-dollar Eisenhower calves.' Missouri farmers, he said, were organizing a 'Never Again Club,' i.e., never again vote Republican. The talk shifted to communism, which, Rayburn agreed, was a threat from outside but not from inside—fascism more of a problem in U.S.

"Tourists mobbed T on Capitol steps. Talked to Osage Indian, from Missouri ('Just as smart as he is fat'). On way back in chauffeured limousine spotted Dean Acheson, striding along. Had driver honk, then swing around and nearly run him down. 'You're the hardest pickup I ever made,' said T, insisting on giving him a lift.

"A: How did you like driving here?

"T: Had a governor on the seat with me. I'd hit it up a little and she'd say, 'How fast are you going?' 'Just fifty-five.' 'You think I'm losing my eyesight? That says sixty-five.' So we'd slow down. Had it up to seventy a few times, but she'd always pull me in.

"Bess and Margaret waiting in suite. Bess had bought a dress and had lunch at a hamburger stand. (Forgot: after press conference this A.M. she said plaintively, 'You're not going to leave me here with all these phones!')

"Talk of Margaret's running for Congress, but T said she'd never be able to get up early enough in the morning."

* * *

Truman was engaged most of Tuesday. My notes resume on Wednesday, Smith's and my last day in Washington:

"June 23. Morning walk with press, taxi- and truck-drivers yelling. 'Hi, Harry! Whatcha doing?' and he yelling back 'Sightseeing!'

"Down to K St., to 14th, Mass. Ave. and return, avoiding White House. Big dinner at night. Hillman showed up with new wife, young and attractive—took a lot of kidding. I sat with them and he introduced me to 'the faithful'—see guest list. Acheson gave main speech, best tribute to T— to almost anybody—I ever heard. Tried to get a copy but couldn't."

The following week the Hearst organization did the honors in New York with a luncheon in a suite of the Waldorf for Truman, his wife, a few guests and the working stiffs. I sat next to Mathew Connelly, his former appointments secretary, who kept me entertained with muttered comments.

"You can have this crowd," he said, meaning his hosts. "We'll take the waiters. They're our people and they'll put us in again next time, don't worry."

Although off a bit on timing, his prophecy seemed to be fulfilled in 1960, when his fellow Massachusetts Irishman beat Nixon.

I saw Truman infrequently after that, several times in the later fifties, when I went out to Independence to ask him for some more articles on various subjects, mostly historical. He obliged with a few, which Warren Hall helped him write. We exchanged a number of letters, among them one which I treasure:

October 31, 1953
Dear Mr. Robbins:

Thanks for your good letter of the 28th. I more than appreciated it and I also appreciated receiving the copyright registration certificates.

I know what you are up against. When the book is finished, I hope you'll find it agreeable to bring it out. I'd like very much to see you again for social reasons and because I like to talk to you.

Sincerely yours,
Harry Truman

Then came a handwritten postscript, reading:

Now that ambiguous sentence up there about the book means that I hope you will find it possible to deliver the picture book [1] to me yourself in person.

---

[1] The "picture book" was a very limited edition, dreamed up and designed by Bradley Smith. It was handmade with original photographic prints made by Smith's assistant, David Brooks, and there were only six copies.

Then to take out more ambiguity I'd like to talk to you about publication of the series "Mr. Citizen" in book form, with some additions. You did so much for the articles.

I had about a dozen more letters from him. One, dated "12/7/56," was in answer to a note of mine in which I'd said that the way things were going it might be a good idea to make Eisenhower king and turn the running of the country over to the Democrats.

"Your suggestion about running the country may be a good one," he replied, "but I'm afraid that having a Roi-Golf might foster excesses similar to those we deplored in the French Revolution."

One or two of his later notes referred rather glumly to getting old. But I was never able to imagine his giving in to age, maybe because when I first met him he already was old in years and at the same time younger in spirit than many of my contemporaries.

His death in December 1972 seemed as unreal to me as the Vietnam deaths we were watching on television at that time. It did not become real until later when I stood beside his grave at the rear of the Truman Library and read the inscription, which he himself had composed:

HARRY S. TRUMAN
Born May 8, 1884
Lamar, Missouri
Died December 26, 1972
Married June 28, 1919
Daughter born February 17, 1924
Judge
Eastern District
Jackson County
Jan. 1, 1923–Jan. 1, 1925
Presiding Judge
Jackson County
Jan. 1, 1927–Jan. 1, 1935
United States Senator
Missouri
Jan. 3, 1935–Jan. 18, 1945
Vice-President
United States
Jan. 20, 1945–Apr. 12, 1945
President
United States
Apr. 12, 1945–Jan. 20, 1953

The words were typical of him. As in his speeches, he just wanted to give the facts.

* * *

When my own retirement started me thinking again about Truman's, I saw his differently from the way I had before. In working with him in 1953, I too had been interested chiefly in the facts: what time he got up, what he did next and so on. He liked this attitude; it fostered our acquaintance more than if I'd been editorializing.

Now, twenty years later, I began really to appreciate what he'd been going through. Recollections of the Washington trip helped, for if I hadn't seen him there, in his element, I'd have had no real way of measuring the amount of change he'd had to adapt to.

In search of the forces, the traits of character, the experiences that had made it possible for him to face up so gracefully to the transformation from most powerful man in the world to private citizen, I reviewed the notes I had made, the recordings, supplementary readings, everything.

An editor friend, to whom I mentioned what I was doing, suggested writing an article about it for his magazine. But the matter did not end there. The magazine piece aroused the interest of a publisher, who asked for a book on the subject. This request prompted another review of the material, and I found some things that had seemed irrelevant to both the original series and the later article.

One day, for instance, I'd asked Truman if he didn't feel that some of his friends had failed him. He was silent for a minute, and I braced myself for a rebuke. But when it came, his answer indicated that the delay had been caused only by an effort to give the question the thought it deserved.

"Yes," he said, "four." And he named them: Byrnes, Henry Wallace, Louis Johnson, and Joseph Grew.

The first three did not surprise me; the last one did. "Grew?" I repeated.

With a pursing of the lips he said, "He was a ladies' man."

I wasn't sure what he meant by the words, but there was no mistaking their finality, and I let the subject drop.

All I knew about Grew at the time was that he had been Ambassador to Japan, then Assistant, or Under, Secretary of State. Later I learned that he was handsome and dashing, Harvard educated and regarded, except by Mr. Truman, as the model of what a diplomat should be. An authority on Truman, to whom I mentioned the incident, smiled and said:

"He had his prudish side—the side that was disgusted with the Folies-Bergère after World War I. Imagine, on his first visit to Paris, after months of dodging shells in all that French mud, he and some buddies take in the Folies-Bergère and he's disgusted!"

Yet I'd noticed that among male friends Truman would contribute his share of locker-room stories and remarks. They even spilled over into mixed company now and then, as indicated by his wife's widely quoted statement about having spent twenty years trying to get him to say manure instead of its colloquial equivalent.

Another time, driving along, he had got onto the subject of Stalin, toward whom his feelings appeared to be ambivalent. "I played poker with him over Iran," he observed. "I called him up and told him if he didn't get his troops out of there inside of a week, I'd bring in three divisions—and the Mediterranean fleet, too. I didn't see how I was going to do it, but I didn't have to. He got out."

And there was the Bomb. Wasn't it true, I asked, that at first so little was known about that kind of weapon that the possibility of its destroying the entire world had had to be taken into account?

Yes, he answered, he had raised the question with the scientists. "They told me that the chance of anything like that happening was only about one in a million. That was good enough for me."

For me, even a one-in-a-million chance of blowing up the world would have been one too many. But he obviously had made up his mind about the Bomb. The necessity of dropping it had become a point of doctrine with him, along with such other points as that the Democratic Party was the party of the people, the Republican the party of privilege, and that, given the facts, the people could be counted on to do the right thing.

With a book in prospect these random confidences no longer were irrelevant. I wanted to find out more about them and about other things he'd said and done, not from books, but from the sources, his and other people's correspondence and diaries and so on, as well as, where possible, from the people themselves. Independence was the obvious place to go, and I decided to make the trip by car as he had liked to do on his quests for information (about roads or courthouses or what the country's mood was).

"You have to get around and listen to what people are saying," he had told me. "Dewey learned that in '48. He didn't listen, he just talked—and didn't say much, either."

So I pursued my quest back to Independence and listened to people who had known Truman, both the living and the dead. A number of the latter, I discovered, had consigned their recollections of him to his library, and what they had to say often turned out to be the more rewarding, for they had unburdened themselves when they were nearer the facts than his few remaining companions are today.

II

World War 1

OF HARRY TRUMAN'S MANY GOOD FRIENDS, THE CLOSEST PERHAPS WERE Edward D. McKim, Harry H. Vaughan and John W. Snyder. Their comradeship had its roots in World War I and its flowering during the postwar summer encampments of the Officers Reserve Corps. McKim was in Captain Truman's Battery D of the 129th Field Artillery, Vaughan, in another regiment of the same division; Snyder also was an artilleryman but attached to a different division.

McKim and Vaughan came together first during their early training days at Camp Doniphan, Fort Sill, Oklahoma.

"I knew Harry Vaughan in 1917," McKim said later. "He was a sergeant in the 128th Field Artillery, which was the St. Louis outfit. Harry had gone to Westminster College and he played football there. He was playing center on the 128th football team and I was playing center on the 129th football team. Some of the fellows on my team had played against Harry in Missouri college ball, so they warned me to look out for him, that he was a pretty tough monkey.

"Harry then probably weighed 200 to 210 pounds; I weighed about 175 pounds. I noticed Harry in practice, and he had a little gimpy leg, had a little drag to it. I thought I'd try out the leg and on the first play I crashed into it and down went Mr. Vaughan. And Mr. Vaughan went down the second time. He got up and he said, 'Look, McKim, I know you've got a bad leg too. You know we're not getting paid for this. Why don't we make a deal? I won't hit you in the leg if you won't hit me in the leg.'

"Well, I started to laugh and we shook hands on it and we've been very close personal friends ever since."

Before this memorable collision, Vaughan had had his first meeting with Harry Truman. He has described it as follows:

"Along about March of 1917, I was a second lieutenant with the 130th Field Artillery.[1] Harry Truman was a first lieutenant with the 129th Field Artillery and up to the day I mention I didn't even know him; I had never seen him. We had a brigade commander by the name of General Lucius Berry. . . . General Berry was a tough old Indian fighter and pretty hard on second lieutenants. He would have a brigade officers' call to which some 150 officers would report . . . and he was always in a hurry. And when he'd get to the meeting, if the officers' call was for three o'clock and he got there at ten minutes to three, he would start the meeting. If you got there at five minutes to three, you were late and you caught the devil.

"On this particular day there were three or four of us walking over to the brigade headquarters, young second lieutenants from the 130th, one of whom was Jim Pendergast of Kansas City.

"We were talking and laughing and as we went through the door, we were clear inside before we realized that the meeting had begun and that General Berry had a young first lieutenant out in front of him, giving him unshirted hell about the way he was running the canteen. It seemed that First Lieutenant Harry Truman, in addition to his other duties, was what we call now PX officer—canteen officer. So, coming through the door we made a lot of noise and Berry was distracted from what he was doing, and he turned and looked us over. We, of course, snapped up to attention and acted like there was nothing the matter at all, and Berry looked right at me. I was the first one in and the biggest and probably making the most noise, and he said, 'What is your name, mister?'

"Well, you may or may not recall that in those days you had to be a first lieutenant before you had any rank; second lieutenants were called mister.

"So, I was standing like a ramrod and I said, 'Vaughan, sir.'

"He said, 'How long have you been an officer in the United States Army?'

"I said, 'Three days, sir,' with which he proceed to go into details as to how he doubted very much if I would ever be an officer in the United States Army if I lived to be a hundred. And while he was giving me the business, much to the amusement of everybody who was behind him, whom he couldn't see, why, this first lieutenant stepped back in the ranks with all the rest of the officers who were standing there, and when Berry got through with me, which took two or three minutes because he really covered the subject, he forgot who he had been talking to and he went on with the meeting. Well, the meeting lasted twenty to thirty minutes and was

[1] Vaughan was transferred to the 130th Field Artillery after his promotion from sergeant to second lieutenant.

instructions about this and that and the other thing, and on the way out, this officer grabbed me by the arm and said, 'Much obliged, mister, you got me off the hook nicely.'

"After we got outside I said, 'Who was that?'

"Jim Pendergast, of course, knew him, because Jim had been in the 129th Regiment before he was commissioned. Jim said, 'Why, that's Lieutenant Harry Truman. He lives in Independence; he's a friend of mine.'

"And that's the first time I ever saw Truman and the first contact I ever had with him."

Vaughan added, "He always kept a grade ahead of me. When I got to be major general, I figured I ranked, except he was Commander in Chief, and I really didn't rank after all."

The 35th Division went abroad in 1918, and from then until the Armistice Vaughan saw little more of Truman. But what he did see impressed him:

"The rest of us would look like bums—mud sticking all over us—and he always looked immaculate, and I was never able to understand why."

The phenomenon had its symbolic aspect. After emerging from the war unmuddied, Truman went on to do the same thing as a stalwart in the ranks of a venal political organization and then again when, as President and former President, he became the target of such master mudslingers as Herbert Brownell (Eisenhower's Attorney General) and Senators McCarthy, Jenner and Nixon.

McKim also has contributed a report of *his* first views of Truman. Soon after arriving in France, Battery D learned that its then commanding officer, Captain John H. Thacher, was being promoted to major and transferred. Truman, who himself had just been made a captain, was put in charge of Battery D.

"He felt," according to McKim, "that . . . the Colonel was trying to break him, because D Battery was kind of a hard battery to handle."

"Dizzy D," as it was called, already had run through two captains besides Thacher. The first had been Charles Allen.

"I thought a lot of Charlie," McKim said, "but Charlie got himself involved with a redheaded woman and our mess fund seemed to disappear. Charlie was cashier of the fund. He went before what they called the Benzine Board and Charlie was washed out of the army. Afterward, he went back to Kansas City. He was the first football coach at Rockhurst College. I played under him. In fact, I was supposed to get twelve dollars a week for going to school, playing center and coaching the line, but I never got the twelve dollars a week."

After Captain Allen came Captain Ritter, an engineer officer, who had been transferred to the field artillery and who did not endear himself to McKim.

"He knew nothing at all about mounted drill, gave the wrong signals and as a result almost got a man killed."

McKim had words with Captain Ritter and was reduced in rank from sergeant to private. Then Ritter was replaced by Thacher and Thacher by Truman.

"I had met Truman in the early days when we were organizing the battery and I didn't care much for him. I didn't care much for the idea of going through a war with a man I considered a sissy, and I began to think of ways and means of transferring out of the outfit, but then I thought all my friends were there and I had better stay with them."

Why had he considered Truman a sissy?

"Just my impression of him at that time. But he certainly after he became captain got me out of that idea real quick. He was the boss of the outfit. He not only commanded it. He owned it."

Truman himself has left a number of accounts of his war experiences, including the brief official one in his *Memoirs*. The sample given below is taken from an undated, handwritten autobiographical sketch, which turned up in his secretary's files. Anyone who spends much time in his library is likely to be struck by the amount of material of this kind he kept dashing off. He may have thought that it would come in handy for speeches, articles and the like. Or it may represent an effort to bring more order to his life or find new meaning in it. Or maybe it was just his way of doodling.

Other segments of the autobiographical sketch will be found in later chapters, identified in each instance by a vertical rule in the left-hand margin.

> When President Wilson declared war on April 16, 1917 . . . I helped to expand Batteries B and C into a regiment. At the organization of Battery F I was elected a 1st Lieutenant.[2] I had not expected to be more than a 2nd Lieut. and would have been happy just to remain a sergeant. I made arrangements for my sister and a good man we had on the farm to take over its operation and I set to work to be a Field Artilleryman sure enough. It was some job. We were drilling every day from early in May as Missouri National Guard until the Federal call on August 5th when we became known as the 129th Field Artillery of the 60th Brigade attached to the 35th Division. From May until August 5, 1917 we were known as the 2nd Mo. Field Artillery.
>
> On Sept. 26, 1917, we arrived at Camp Doniphon located just west of and adjoining Ft. Sill, Okla. My duties really piled up after we arrived at Camp.

[2] It was the custom then to elect first lieutenants as well as some other officers.

Not only was it expected of me to do regular duty as a 1st Lieutenant in Battery F but the Colonel made me regimental canteen officer. I'd had no experience in merchandising, so I persuaded Capt. Pete Allen who commanded Battery F to let me get Sgt. Edward Jacobson assigned to me to operate the canteen. We then got orders issued that each battery headquarters company and supply company would assign one man to work at the canteen after drill hours. For this they received an extra dollar a day from canteen profits. We also had the battery barbers all assigned to the canteen. They charged a quarter for a haircut and a dime for a shave and were allowed to keep 40% of what they took in. The rest went to the canteen fund. We also set up a tailor shop where the men could have their uniforms fitted for a small sum. The tailor was also on a percentage basis. All these men had to do military duty as well as work at the canteen.

In order to get started we suggested to the Regimental Commander that he order each Battery and Hqus. and Supply Co. to turn over to the Canteen Officer from their respective mess funds a sum equal to $2.00 per man. There were eleven hundred men in the regiment so Sgt. Jacobson and I had $2200.00 as a capital fund with which to start business. After six months operation we'd paid to the various mess funds $10,000.00 in dividends and their original investment had been returned. We had a stock on hand of about $5,000.00. Our overhead was low, our prices were bedrock and we had no credit accounts. The service at our canteen was so good that adjoining regiments were also our patrons. Most canteen officers had trouble with their accounts and got sent home or court martialed. Jacobson and I had good luck, we kept our accounts carefully, insisted on a monthly audit, and the canteen Officer [3] was recommended for promotion to Captain and was sent overseas with the Division advance school detail on March 20, 1918. . . .

After I'd gone to a couple of schools overseas and had served six weeks as Captain and Adjutant of the 2nd Battalion of the 129th F.A. under Major Marvin H. Gates I was ordered to take over the command of Battery D. This Battery was considered the Regimental Problem Battery. It had had four [4] commanding officers, two of whom were very capable officers and excellent soldiers. The Colonel had considered breaking it up and creating another outfit by transferring its personnel to the other batteries and filling it in by transfer from the other outfits.

They called themselves the Irish Battery and it did sound as if the Hibernians were meeting when the roll was called, except that now and then along with the McKims and the Caseys and the Donnellys there'd be a Schmidt and a Weisburger. Most of the men were from De La Salle High School and Rockhurst College, a couple of fine Catholic schools in Kansas City. There were only seven or eight Protestants in the outfit and when I took command I was one of the seven or eight.

---

[3] I.e., Truman himself.
[4] Three by the count of McKim and several Truman biographers.

I've been very badly frightened several times in my life, and the morning of July 11, 1918 when I took over that Battery was one of those times. I was most anxious to make good in my new role of Captain and I was rather doubtful of my ability to handle that obstreperous battery.

For some reason or other we hit it off and they went to the front Aug. 18, 1918 under my command and were brought home and discharged May 6, 1919 [5] and all their discharges were signed by me. They took up a collection and bought me a big silver cup with a most beautiful inscription on it and they all continue to call me Captain Harry. . . .

A sergeant named Ed Sandifer enlightened Battery D about its new captain. A blacksmith (a necessary component of the horse-and-mule-drawn field artillery of those days), Sandifer had served in another battery with Truman, and he was not the sort to mistake a sissy for a non-sissy. He placed his former comrade squarely in the second category, a judgment Truman himself soon confirmed.

There was, for instance, the often-related story of the "Battle of Who Run," when the men panicked under fire and their captain turned them around with a stream of words many of them had not believed he knew.

And there was the episode at Chepy. Truman, as he often did, had moved forward, alone, to spy out the enemy positions.

"While he was out there," McKim said, "we were strafed by a couple of German planes. They came over, and the German would lean out of the plane and throw these potato-mashers at us—these grenades that looked like potato-mashers, had a handle on them."

As soon as Truman got back to the battery, "he gave orders to hitch up and pull out. We got up the road probably a hundred yards and where we had just left, boy, the shells were just raining in there. We would have been caught, but we were a hundred yards away by that time—just intuition on his part that we got out of there."

Next day, as another result of his lonely reconnaissance, Battery D destroyed one German battery and put two others out of commission. Instead of being decorated, as his men thought he—and they—deserved to be, Truman nearly got court-martialed for firing outside his sector.

But his exploits in the field were not the only reason for the esteem in which his men held him. They also liked the way he treated them. A sergeant, Frederick J. Bowman, has something to say about that.

When he joined up in 1915, Bowman, an outstanding basketball player, somehow had the illusion that playing on his outfit's basketball team was all that would be required of him. It came as a rude surprise when he was ordered into action in Mexico.

[5] Battery D under Truman's command did not suffer a single casualty.

The election in [41] the Fall of 1934 was a pushover for the Democrats. So I came to the United States Senate and went to work, — I was in luck on Committee assignments — Interstate Commerce, Appropriations and a couple of minor ones — Printing and Public Buildings and Grounds. Senator Wheeler was Chairman of Interstate Commerce and Senator Glass was Chairman of Appropriations. Wheeler had succeeded in getting a resolution through the Senate authorizing the Interstate Commerce Committee or any subcommittee thereof to investigate the financial transactions of the Railroads. That subcommittee, of which Wheeler appointed himself chairman began its deliberations along in the fall of 1935. Being interested in transportation and communications I attended the meetings of the subcommittee. Wheeler saw that I was interested and finally made me one of the subcommittee members, and later its vice chairman. Sitting as a "hearing committee" is a dull boresome proceedure and it requires patience and persistance. So I soon became the "patient and persistant" member of the Subcommittee of the Interstate Commerce Committee on RR. Finance.

A page from Mr. Truman's
handwritten autobiography

This may be the only time Harry Truman was ever seen in Washington in his shirt-sleeves. He is arriving at the Mayflower Hotel on June 20, 1953; it is his first trip back to the capital as a private citizen. The ex-President has just driven 1050 miles from Independence, Missouri, tak-ing two and a half days for the trip. He and Bess had planned to make the journey incognito, but, according to Truman, the slow speed at which Bess forced him to drive caused them to be recognized all along the way.

Truman lost no time in getting his shirt-sleeves covered; his first act after greeting the doorman was to put on his double-breasted suit jacket. Then Harry Truman, like any other traveler, carefully supervised the unloading of his car. Even though it had been a long, hot drive, Truman was his usual ebullient self.

In this rare photograph Bess Truman, usually very reserved in public, has a big smile on as she is welcomed back to Washington by her daughter Margaret and a coterie of Washington acquaintances. Both in Independence and in Washington I found her to be cooperative and pleasant, with a highly developed sense of humor.

After his early-morning walk, the former President stopped at the Capitol to chat with an Osage Indian who wanted to shake his hand and wish him well. Truman had the knack of making the people he met feel that he was truly glad to see them—and he usually was.

Four out of five of these tourists visiting Washington were thrilled to meet the friendly ex-President unexpectedly. But one little girl was too shy even to look at Mr. Truman. Her blond grandmother held on to the President's hand and did not want to let go. Within seconds other tourists were arriving on the scene to greet him.

Never hurt anyone's feelings if it can be avoided, was Truman's creed. And it extended to photographers and reporters. Asked to pose against the Capitol dome, the ex-President readily agreed, but added, "You probably don't know that this building was occupied in 1863 before the rebuilding was finished and it has never been properly completed."

Happy to see so many of the White House correspondents and photographers, Truman took time out for a brief press conference. Among other things, he commented on the newly introduced *Democratic Digest*. Then he personally greeted the photographers and reporters and proved that he remembered the men by calling them by their first names. At the end of the session he said, "Now how about letting me hear the most used phrase in photography—just one more!"

After a morning walk in Washington we took a taxi to the Washington Monument, since I wanted to photograph the former President there. During the drive I asked Mr. Truman if he hadn't come in for a lot of criticism during his last Administration. "To tell the truth," he said, "I didn't care what they called me as long as it wasn't unprintable."

Gesticulating with both hands, David Stowe, Truman's former administrative aide, makes a point at lunch with his former chief. The man in the middle is General Harry Vaughan, also a veteran of World War I, a close personal friend of Truman, his military aide as Vice-President, and later his aide as President. Vaughan occasionally got into trouble because of his penchant for practical jokes: he was often referred to as the Administration's court jester.

The ex-President discusses a forthcoming speech with his former research specialist, David Lloyd, who had worked in the State Department under Adlai Stevenson before being invited to join Truman's staff.

(*Right*) Famous men from Missouri meet at a Capitol lunch hosted by Representative Clarence Cannon (right) and Speaker Sam Rayburn (Texas). By the time of this luncheon, the man on the far left, Stuart Symington, had become a senator with Truman's support. During the war years, Symington headed the National Security Resources Board. Clarence Cannon was chairman of the powerful House Appropriations Committee. Sam Rayburn was Speaker of the House of Representatives. This was a happy, and at times even hilarious, reunion.

(*Below right*) Cannon and Truman had great respect for one another. They had much in common: both were from small towns, both were history buffs. Cannon had started out as a lawyer, then became a history professor at Stephens College in Columbia, Missouri. He served in Congress for a total of twenty-six years.

(*Below far right*) Sam Rayburn and the ex-President had been friends since Truman became Senator. They had often met in the anteroom of Rayburn's office (sometimes known as "the Board of Education") for a bourbon and water. It was there one day in 1945 that Vice-President Truman got a call from Roosevelt's Press Secretary, Steve Early, requesting that he hurry to the White House. There Mrs. Roosevelt told him the President was dead. "I went over there to see what I could do for the President. When I got there I *was* the President." Rayburn had been at the first luncheon Truman attended as President on April 13, 1945.

This was the last meeting of the Truman brain trust, or "my crew," as he called them, its purpose to work on a speech he was to deliver that week to a reserve officers group. From left to right: Don Dawson, administrative assistant; Mathew J. Connelly, appointments secretary; David Lloyd, research assistant; Charles Murphy, special counsel to the President; Jim Sundquist, special assistant to the President in matters of defense mobiliza-

tion; and David Stowe, economist. All
had been helpful in getting the President
elected in 1948.

Truman bounced his speech ideas off
these men. They often provided the design or framework for his talk, but the
end product was clearly Truman's—his
thoughts and his style, never elegant, always simple and sincere and, as he often
said, with no "two-dollar words."

As we drove along the streets of the capital, Truman suddenly shouted, "Pull up, there's a friend of mine," and leaped out to greet Dean Acheson. For the next five minutes they held an unofficial street-corner conference, both obviously moved to see one another. It would have been difficult to find two Americans who were

more different in background and temperament; yet they were fast friends, deeply dedicated to the principles of democratic government. Truman depended upon Acheson's judgment and insight in foreign affairs, but made his own final decisions.

In preparation for a telecast, the ex-President and Margaret were asked to sit on the arms of a chair with Bess in the middle. Bess was not too anxious to do the program; she said nobody would want to see her. Mr. Truman said that he and Margaret would take care of that and leaned in, hiding Bess from the cameras. All three broke up at this and it took the camera technicians another five minutes to set the scene.

The former President spoke while Bess and Margaret listened intently. It was a brief informal talk, describing his return to Washington as an ordinary citizen.

As soon as the camera lights went off, everyone was smiling, relieved to have the session finished. By 1953 Margaret probably had as much television experience as her father. He considered her a professional. She had appeared on Ed Sullivan's *Toast of the Town* show, among others, and was making her debut as an actress. A year after this picture was taken she was guest host for Edward R. Murrow and, from New York, interviewed her family, who were at home in Independence.

On his return, he made a determined effort to have done with the military but succeeded only in arousing the ire of his commanding officer, a Captain Elliot. Next thing he knew he, his Battery D and Elliot, now promoted to lieutenant colonel of the 129th Field Artillery, were being shipped to France. Thenceforth he was periodically recommended for promotion and each time Elliot would cross him off the list.

Truman, after taking over the battery, decided that Bowman deserved to go to officer training school. Bowman said he appreciated the thought but the captain would just get in bad with Colonel Elliot.

"I've been up before," he explained, "and I've been more or less blackballed, you might say, and that's perfectly all right with me. The war isn't going to last forever, and I'd just as soon not do it."

Truman refused to be deterred. "You're entitled to it," he said. "You should have had it a long time ago." And he promised to take the case to General Berry if necessary. In fact, he finally did succeed in getting Bowman sent to the school, from which he was graduated a few days before the war ended.

"That," said Bowman some years afterward, "demonstrated in my opinion the position he has taken in the later years on the different things that he felt were fair and just and he didn't care who bothered about them; if it was right, he was going to push it through. . . . And I think that was one of the main characteristics of the man."

Bowman's last recollections of his D days were of the loving cup (purchased with money collected from crap games) which the battery presented to Truman, and of a review of the troops by the Prince of Wales.

"We had a little kid by the name of Johnny Higinbotham, had to stand on his tiptoes to get in, he's only about that high. And we were over at Commercy, in France, and there was going to be a review there by the Prince . . . with General Pershing and everybody—and oh, we had what they called dub enamel. It was a kind of wax that you put on your shoes and then you'd brush it and shine it. And we worked and everything had to be spic-and-span and clean. And we got out there and, oh, it just poured rain, and this field . . . was sopping wet. So, you sit out there in water for a couple of hours and finally (they were slow in coming along) and finally they did come along and [we] opened ranks for them, for the Prince to come down there and it was just as he got by us, this little Higinbotham in the back end says, 'Captain, ask that little son of a bitch when he's going to free Ireland.'

"Here was General Pershing, and here was the major general of the division and the colonel of the regiment and finally poor old Captain

Truman along with them, when this guy blurted that out. Well, that was typical of Battery D."

Harry Truman had a lot of reasons to skip World War I and, in fact, could have done so without laying himself open to criticism. He was thirty-three years old and the sole support of his mother and sister—his father, John Anderson Truman, had died by then and his younger brother, Vivian, was married and living on a farm of his own. He had at last succeeded in getting engaged to Bess Wallace, the girl he'd been courting most of his life; he was deep in an oil-drilling venture, which he discontinued and which, he learned later, would have made him rich if he'd kept on with it. He was leaving the family farm in the uncertain care of his sister and a hired man. And he had bad eyesight.

Although Truman's two boyhood health crises have been written about many times, they had such an effect on his development that it is impossible to attempt a picture of him without mentioning them. His eye condition caused the first, and diphtheria, which he came down with at age nine, the second. His brother Vivian also got diphtheria but recovered quickly; his sister escaped it.

Harry nearly died. Then, after getting over the disease, he went on suffering the aftereffects. He was paralyzed for six months. His mother had to wheel him around in a baby carriage, and for a while he was dangerously accident-prone.

Martha Ellen Truman was too sensible a parent to favor one of her children over the other two, yet her elder son's misfortunes inevitably brought her closer to him than to his brother and sister. The family balance was disturbed: John Anderson and Vivian were nudged together and Mary Jane was left in the center, a little princess, waited on by all the menfolk. She later remarked that she guessed the reason she never married was that her brothers had spoiled her for ordinary beaux.

Harry was about five when it dawned on Martha Ellen that there was something wrong with his eyes; previously he had seemed to get around well enough and he could read fairly large print, such as that in the family Bible. Now she discovered that smaller letters were a blur to him. A doctor diagnosed the trouble as flat eyeballs, a condition necessitating a lifelong dependence on glasses.

Children did not wear eyeglasses in those days, only adults did. So at a stroke Harry Truman became a curiosity, a kind of freak. He could not roughhouse and play games the way other kids did; he might break his glasses. He had to be careful, and being careful made him seem to be not only a freak but a sissy.

People have been crippled psychologically for life by childhood experiences no more traumatic than those of Truman's. In the effort to prove that he was not a sissy he might have turned into the then equivalent of a juvenile delinquent, another Huck Finn. Instead, he let his mother lead him into music and reading. Neither pursuit narrowed the gap between him and his fellows, yet he worked hard at both and got real pleasure from them, especially books. History and biography were his favorite subjects; he loved to read about battles and generals; they helped to compensate for what he was missing.

But being by nature a doer rather than a dreamer, he also acted out as many of his fancies as he could. Even before his National Guard days —during the Spanish-American War—he got a taste of military life by joining a local junior militia, which drilled, camped in the woods and, in his words, "had a grand time."

But how was anyone with eyesight as poor as his ever able to get into the regular army? After tracking the question unsuccessfully through his *Memoirs* and a number of books about him I finally ran it to ground in Independence. Half of the answer appears in a questionnaire which was submitted to Truman when he was President and now is on file in his library. The document is undated and, aside from the conclusions to be drawn from its contents, unidentified. It reads in part:

"There are several published references to the President's eye defect, that it kept him out of West Point. One account says he persuaded an examining sergeant to whisper the letters to him and thus enable him to pass the Army examinations for World War I service. Correct?"

Truman's reply is handwriten: "Have a flat eyeball (far-sighted). National Guard physical not so strict as regular army. Secretary of War ordered a one-eyed Lieutenant and myself passed in 129th Field Artillery. Artillery men were hard to get. Later on when promoted it took some maneuvering."

Fred Truman, second of Vivian's four sons, was able to throw some light on the word "maneuvering."

"Uncle Harry memorized the eye-test chart," he told me. "Some fellow had memorized it first and made a copy and then *he* memorized it. He couldn't see without his glasses even to tell where it was.

"He took six pairs of glasses with him when he went to France, and he came back with all six. Once he was riding his horse and a limb of a tree knocked a pair right off his nose. He looked around and there they were on his horse's rump. . . ."

Harry Truman was what you might call a highly motivated soldier.

III

An Educated Man

When I graduated from High School in May 1901 it was expected by the family and by me that there would be some chance for more education. Difficulties overtook us, which resulted in the loss of the family farm of 160 acres and of the home place at Waldo and River Blvd. in Independence. It was necessary that some addition be made to the family income. So I got a job as timekeeper on a railroad construction outfit under L. J. Smith. He was building a double track for the Sante Fe Railroad from a little place named Eton to Sheffield, a suburb of Kansas City. My salary was $35 a month and board. There were three construction camps about five miles apart. It was my job to check the men at each of these camps twice daily. I was furnished with a tricycle car. Its power was by hand and I furnished the power.

The workmen were hobos and they worked from payday to payday to get enough money for one weekend drunk. Payday was every two weeks. If a man drew his pay under the two weeks he was discounted ten percent. Daily pay was fifteen cents an hour for ten hours a day. A team and dump wagon received thirty-five cents an hour for ten hours a day. Blacksmiths, cooks and specialists received seventeen and one-half cents an hour or a dollar seventy-five a day.

On Saturday, every two weeks, I sat in some saloon either in Independence or Sheffield and signed checks for all who'd worked two weeks and who wanted to be paid off. Some of the men only drew pay once a month or sometimes once in six months. These men were very few in number and were usually farmers who owned teams and wagons. They saved their money. Hobos only used money for one purpose—to buy whiskey at the bar where the check was cashed until all the money was gone. After the bi-weekly libation was slept off most of 'em were back on the job Monday morning to start in for another two weeks.

After working some eight or ten months for the railroad contractor the job ended by being completed and I went to work for the Kansas City Star "wrapping singles" in the mailing department at nine dollars a week—a raise in pay. Then one of my friends came along early in 1903 or late in 1902 and I went to work in the basement of the National Bank of Commerce at 10th and Walnut, Kansas City, Mo., as a clerk at $35 a month. At that time we lived at 2108 Park Avenue in Kansas City. My brother and I worked at the bank and my father worked at an elevator in the east bottoms. In 1904 my father traded the house at 2108 Park for an equity in 80 acres in Henry County, Mo., and late in 1904 the family moved to Clinton. I went to board at 1314 Troost Avenue with some of the bank boys. A good woman named Trow ran the boarding house. We lived two in a room, and paid $5.00 a week for room, breakfast and dinner. For lunch we paid ten cents to a box lunch place on east 8th Street—and we stayed in good condition physically, too. Mrs. Trow was a cook you read about but seldom see and the box lunch was a balanced ration before vitamins were ever heard of.

Early in 1905 I quit the National Bank of Commerce and went to work for the Union National Bank. I'd improved my financial position in the National Bank of Commerce by some twenty-five dollars a month. But the Union National gave me $75.00 a month to do exactly the same kind of work I was doing at the Commerce for $60.00, so I moved. It was a much pleasanter place to work. The chief clerk and the V.P. in charge of the help at the Union National were kind and sympathetic while the chief clerk and the V.P. at the Commerce were just the opposite.

The Vice-President at the Commerce, who hired and fired the help, was a fellow named Charles H. Moore. His job was to give the official balling out. He was an artist at it. He could have humiliated the nerviest man in the world. Anyway all the boys in the Commerce Zoo were afraid of him as were all the tellers and bookkeepers. He was never so happy as when he could call some poor inoffensive little clerk up before him in the grand lobby of the biggest bank west of the Mississippi and tell him how dumb and inefficient he was because he'd sent a check belonging in the remittance of the State Bank of Oakland, Kans. to Ogden, Utah. He would always remember that trivial mistake when the clerk asked for a raise. . . .

I wasn't long at the Union National Bank until I was getting $100.00 a month, a magnificent salary in Kansas City in 1905. In June of that year Captain George R. Collins decided to start a National Guard Battery of light artillery in Kansas City. Some of the boys in the bank were going into it. I was twenty-one years old in May of that year and I could do as I pleased. So I joined the battery. After reading all the books obtainable in the Independence and Kansas City libraries on history and government from Egypt to U.S.A. I came to the conclusion that every citizen should know something about military, finance or banking and agriculture. All my heros [sic] or great leaders were somewhat familiar with one or the other or all three. So I started my grass roots military education by joining a National Guard Battery June 14, 1905. In August we went on our first encampment at Cape Girardeau, Mo. It was quite an experience. We went to St. Louis in a day coach on the Missouri Pacific and then by steamboat down the Mississippi. I learned a lot about public relations and private ones too. There were several camps after that one—at St. Joseph where we camped in three feet of water in the fair grounds and a tent was struck by lightning killing a man or two—at Ft. Riley, Kans., where I was made a corporal. I still have the warrant framed. It was the biggest promotion I ever recieved [sic] and I've had 'em all up to Colonel and Vice-President of the U.S.A.

After the family moved to Clinton, I spent week ends down there and at the old home farm at Grandview, where my maternal grandmother and the old bachelor uncle for whom I was named lived. The uncle wanted to move back to town so he made a proposition to my father and mother to come back to the old home place and live. I took the word to them and urged them to move. They agreed to accept and I agreed to quit the bank and go to work on the farm if they did move. . . .

THE ABOVE NARRATIVE IS AS INTERESTING FOR ITS OMISSIONS AS FOR WHAT the author saw fit to include. For example, he has scarcely anything to say about Kansas City, which at that time was one of the most colorful towns in the country. The Pendergast political machine was coming into power then, and if there was one thing the Pendergast brothers were not it was prudish. They liked to see people have a good time on the simple principle that a happy man could be depended on to spend more money than an unhappy one. The principle operated in their favor, they reasoned, and it operated automatically; all they did was expedite it a little by supplying those immemorial props of happiness, saloons and brothels.

In the midst of their rambunctious metropolis was Harry Truman, self-described as "twenty-one years old" with "a magnificent salary" and able to "do as I pleased." And what did he do? Work hard at his job, read books on history and government, join the National Guard and now and then treat another bank clerk to a weekend of his mother's cooking at the family's new farm. The closest he came to what the Pendergasts might have called fun was spare-time ushering at the Grand Theater (where he got a free look at the major vaudeville acts of the period) and playing practical jokes on fellow boarders.

One of the jokes, famous by now, began at a picnic. A couple of the young men present put a note in a bottle and floated it down the Missouri River. Harry and other pranksters persuaded some friends in Mississippi to play the part of two romantic girls, who supposedly had received the note and were answering it. An increasingly amorous correspondence ensued and went on until the joke was exposed.

Meanwhile, John Anderson Truman was finding little to joke about. Besides his preferred occupation, cattle trading (less preferred, farming), he also had a taste for speculation. The last had resulted in the "difficulties" mentioned earlier. Plunging in grain futures and real estate, he had lost about $30,000 cash and most of his landed property, including his pleasant home in Independence and a 160-acre farm his wife recently had inherited from her father.

As we know, the Trumans had then moved into a cheap Kansas City house, and John Anderson, the jaunty cattleman manqué, had tasted the bitterness of having to work as a night watchman in a grain elevator. Of the three separate failures he had suffered since the birth of his elder son, that of 1901 was the worst, yet you hardly would guess so from the elder son's account of it. Nor does that account begin to suggest the son's feelings at being suddenly cut off from the thing he had been best at—education, book learning.

Different from other boys because of his glasses, he evidently had told himself, all right, he'd *be* different, but in a way that would compel respect. He'd be a scholar, an authority; and, in fact, he had managed to fit himself into that difficult role. His family, teachers, friends all had begun to look on him as a prodigy, who could settle arguments and quote from the Good Book by the yard.

One of his lifelong companions, Henry Chiles, recalls him at the age of eleven:

"He moved to the opposite corner of the block. He was on Waldo Street and I'm on White Oak and the alley ran between, and that was our town meeting grounds in between the two places. That's where we played, up and down that alley. We'd be playing cowboy or shinny or any game we played—those are all pretty rough—rougher than the games they play now—and Harry would come by. I didn't get acquainted with him right away—his brother played with us, but he did not play much in those rough games because he wore double-strength glasses. He just couldn't get in that kind of a game.

"Once in a while they would kid him, but he was serious. They wanted to call him a sissy, but they just didn't do it because they had a lot of respect for him. I remember one time we were playing, I think, another game we played, Jesse James or robbers, and we were the Dalton Brothers out in Kansas—that's about the time they got killed—and we were arguing about them. Harry came by—we got the history mixed up ourselves—but Harry straightened it out, just who were the Dalton brothers and how many got killed. Things like that the boys had a lot of respect for. . . ."

Ethel Noland, Harry's first cousin and the family historian, said of those same days: "He was always the teacher's pet, because he was a very fine little boy, a very good little boy, I must say, really the best little boy in the whole family connection and possibly the best one in his room wherever he went to school."

And Mrs. W. L. C. Palmer, his high school Latin and math teacher, whom I talked to in 1953, observed with pride:

". . . It was something going on in Congress that they didn't approve of, and Chief Justice Vinson said, 'Well, like old Cato said in the Roman senate, "It ought to be destroyed, Carthage ought to be destroyed, Carthago delenda est." ' And Harry said, 'You didn't say that right. You should have said, "Delenda est Carthago." ' "

She also remembered how pleased she had been when Harry and Dr. Twyman's son, Elmer, and Charlie Ross, who later became Harry's Press Secretary, had devoted some of their afternoons to building a bridge on the model of one they had read about in class, in Caesar's Commentaries.

And now, after graduation, here was her promising student, through no fault of his own, consorting with hoboes, wrapping newspapers and adding up figures in the basement of a bank. Of course, he performed these humble tasks as well as he had his Latin (the foreman of the construction gang had been moved to say, "Harry's all right—from the navel on out in every direction"), but still . . .

His hopes of continuing his formal education revived briefly when it occurred to him that either Annapolis or West Point might be a possibility; they were tuition-free. He started to study for them only to learn that his eyesight barred him from any chance of being accepted. This blow must have been especially painful as he watched Charlie Ross and Elmer Twyman go off to their colleges.

But he gave no sign of resentment, unless stopping his piano lessons was one. Thoughts of the expense probably dimmed his hopes of a musical career, but he has been quoted as saying that taking piano lessons was "a sissy thing to do."

It's plain, though, that he was not sulking or otherwise expressing resentment, for he kept on with his reading and, so far as possible, with his other interests. To help his parents, he was merely—and uncomplainingly—forgoing the burgeoning advantages of city life. And in the same spirit he came to accept the idea that the rest of his education, if there were to be any, would have to be self-administered. These decisions were not as momentous as a lot of the ones he had to make later, but they revealed an uncommonly mature view of the world.

Bearing them in mind, it's nice today, in going through his library, to stumble on evidence that in the long run he did as well by himself educationally as might have been the case if he had gone to college. Consider, for instance, the following reminiscence of his last Secretary of State, Dean Acheson: [1]

"In August 1946, or late July, the Russians had sent a note to Turkey that they wanted to horn in on the defense of the straits, and they sent a copy to us, the French and the British. They said the Treaty of Montreux had to be reviewed in connection with the joint defense of the straits. I was Acting Secretary; Jimmy [Byrnes] was away. I notified the President about this and got together with the Defense people.

"We worked very hard on this. Patterson was Secretary of War and Forrestal the Secretary of the Navy. We had a couple of meetings. And two or three days later we went over it with the Chiefs of Staff. There was no chairman then. Eisenhower was the Chief of Staff of the Army, and Tooey Spaatz, I think, was Chief for the Air Force. I can't remember for the life of me who the Navy man was.

"We studied the whole business, and it seemed to us that this was critical. We recommended to the President that we tell the Turks we would stand by them. Once the Russians got into the straits, the Turks would be gone, the whole eastern Mediterranean would be gone. When we had got all this worked out, we all went over—there was quite a crowd, the Secretaries and the Chiefs. We met in the President's study. I was the spokesman, and I told him what we had done, what the conclusion was.

"The President asked two or three questions. Then he said, 'I approve. Go ahead.' There was no big talk like this talk on Formosa. Eisenhower sat beside me, and it was all over in a short time. He was very worried. He said, 'Do you think the President really understands what's really going on?' I said, 'Yes, but the only way to find out is to ask him.'

"The President saw us talking and asked, 'Are there any questions?' And the General, or I, said, 'We just want to be sure you understand the full implication of this.' The President laughed and pulled open a drawer of his desk. He took out a big folder, black, with a great big map of the eastern Mediterranean and the Middle East. It had cellophane over it. There were, there was a whole series of these. He put this out and gave us a ten-minute lecture on the strategic importance of the eastern Mediterranean and the Middle East. I turned to Ike and I said, 'Are you satisfied?' And he said, 'O.K.'

"Another time we went up to the dedication of the U.N. building, my

[1] Contributed by Acheson during the preparation of Truman's *Memoirs*.

wife and I went up in the Presidential car [Pullman, not motor]. There was Mrs. Truman, and we had quite a group of Congressional people going up there. We had quite a day, and then we came back at the end of the afternoon. We had lost everyone except the President and Mrs. Truman and my wife. No, Mrs. Truman was going to stay up there with Margaret. So, there were three of us alone in the car.

"We had dinner. It was late in the afternoon. For almost the whole trip from New York we sat at the table because my wife, towards the end of dinner, began talking about Central Asia. I think she had just read a book—Fitzroy McClean's (?)—the English edition was called *Eastern Approaches*.

"Well, that got him started. They cleared away the dishes, and he took the back end of a fork and began to lecture on the history of Central Asia, the various emperors, the migrations of the populations, the Khans. He followed military campaigns, mass migrations, all over the place.

"Towards the end of this my wife said, 'This is amazing. I wouldn't have been surprised that you would know all about the Civil War, but this part of the world, I've never known anyone in my life who knew anything about it.'

"He said, 'Well, my eyesight isn't any good. I was never any good at playing games where you have to see what you're doing at a distance. I couldn't see a ball if it hit me in the nose, so I spent my time reading. The library was not too good where we lived, but it had books, and I guess I read during that period nearly every book in the library. I got interested in this part of the world and ever since I've read everything about it I could find. I'm not a scholar. I know I read the wrong books, but I read a lot, and I suppose I got some good ones now and then.'

"Well, no one could have given you a more fascinating lecture, or a more perceptive one. It was not a lot of unconnected events; you could see why these people were moving around, what the pressures were, what was pushing them. You could see the sort of seething of human life over this vast area. I was fascinated. . . ."

Praise from Caesar, it's said, is praise indeed, and educationally speaking, Acheson, a graduate of Groton, Yale and Harvard Law School (with a stint as secretary to U.S. Supreme Court Justice Louis Brandeis), was a kind of Caesar.

> So in 1906 we all moved to the old home place at Grandview.[2] My grandmother was 88 years old at the time but as hale and hearty as a woman of fifty. She was a grand old lady. Had helped make my grandfather a suc-

[2] The clincher in persuading John Anderson Truman to move was not his son's urging but the fact that a flood had wiped out his whole corn crop.

cessful man.[3] She was a good Baptist, a strong sympathiser with the Confederate States of America and an Indian fighter on her own. She has told me a great many stories of conditions in Jackson County in the 1840's. My grandfather ran a wagon train from Westport and Independence to Salt Lake City and San Francisco from 1844 to the late sixties and my grandmother kept the five thousand acre Jackson County farms going. She not only raised her own children—seven of them to be grown—two died as children—but she raised a couple of nephews and numerous slave children and neighbor orphans. She had the most beautiful red hair I've ever seen and a kindly, benevolent attitude to those she liked. If she didn't like a person, he didn't have any difficulty in finding it out. She was kind and considerate to those who worked for her but she stood for no foolishness and she had a way of keeping people in their proper places which I've never seen equalled. For instance, after I'd joined the Missouri National Guard in 1905 I went out one week end to show her my new Guard uniform—beautiful blue with red stripes down the trouser legs and red piping on the cuffs and a red fouregere [sic] over the shoulder. She looked me over and I knew I was going to catch it. She said: "Harry, this is the first time since 1863 that a blue uniform has been in this house. Don't bring it here again." I didn't.

In the difficulties along the Missouri-Kansas border old Jim Lane,[4] a Kansas hero, had burned her house, killed four hundred of her hogs, cut the hams out and let the carcasses lie to rot. On top of that he forced her to make biscuits for the men until all her fingers were blistered. Old Jim was on his way to plunder and rob Oseola, Missouri, at that time. That caused Quantrill to go to Lawrence for reprisals. Old Jim's a hero in the history books and Quantrill's a villain. It all depends on who writes the histories. The Adamses and the New England historians made a crook and atheist out of Thomas Jefferson until honest research proved 'em in error (to put it mildly). I'm off the subject. . . .

Interviewed in 1965, Ethel Noland, second of three daughters of one of John Anderson Truman's three sisters, talked about the family's background and how she happened to be an authority on the subject:

"I have two filing cases full of letters from him, mostly after he was President, but what he wrote about was largely family history. They began to worry him when he was elected Senator about his ancestry, who he was, what kind of people were the Trumans? Of course, the reports were exaggerated: he was a nobody, he was nothing, he was poor, he was ignorant, he was stupid, he was just a lot of things that he wasn't. And so this question of who he was began to come up, and he would write and say, 'Well, who am I?' 'Am I kin to this one, that one, or the other one?'

[3] Truman's maternal grandfather, Solomon Young, died in 1893.
[4] Lane was a pro-Union militiaman, later U.S. Senator from Kansas. William Clarke Quantrill's band of Confederate guerillas included Jesse James and his brother, Frank.

And he began to get countless letters from people who were named Truman and all of that; and the people in Kentucky where our families had lived wrote to him: 'Did he come from the Youngs of Shelby County?'—the Greggs, the Trumans, the Holmeses, the Tylers?—all that great raft of people that anybody's kin to, you know, and was he kin to them? Well, he didn't know, he didn't know who he was kin to. 'Well, Ethel Noland knows, I'll ask her.' And letter followed letter, and we're still writing.

"And that's what I'm trying to fill in, about these things that I would know, that nobody on earth but me, now, would know. My sisters never paid much attention to those family records. In fact, I'm the only one of us that did. There's always one in every family that will do these things, and the rest sometimes tolerate it, but they generally think it's rather dry stuff; so it's depended on me to tell whom we're kin to and whom we're not kin to and all that. The family legends, someway, are locked up in my mind and—I don't know whether it's a talent or a vice but some people have that sort of failing. Harry Truman said of himself that he had more useless junk in his mind that nobody cared anything about than any person in the world; well, I think I'm just another one that has a little different kind of junk in my mind. It's like an old attic that needs cleaning out. . . ."

According to Ethel, there were two main branches of the Truman family in this country, both offshoots of Trumans who owned one of England's biggest breweries, in Nottingham. Harry's and her forebears, she believed, had emigrated more or less directly to Kentucky, whence in the early nineteenth century they moved westward. The other migrant Trumans settled in New England.

Ethel's—and Harry's—maternal grandmother, Mary Jane Holmes, trekked to Missouri with her family. Then she returned alone to Kentucky, where, without her widowed mother's consent, she married Anderson Shippe Truman. A farmer and schoolteacher, Anderson Shippe started worrying about what they'd done—or rather about the way they'd done it. Finally to relieve his mind he saddled up and by himself rode all the way to Missouri to ask his mother-in-law's forgiveness.

When she gave it, he retraced his steps, collected his bride and chattels and went back to Missouri, where he settled down. Mary Jane Holmes was a collateral descendant of John Tyler, the first U.S. Vice-President to become President on the death of his predecessor in office (William Henry Harrison).

The Anderson Shippe Trumans had three daughters and two sons, and the younger son, John Anderson, was Harry's father. He was "very tiny as a baby," Ethel says. His nickname was Peanuts.

While he and his brothers and sisters were children, the novels of Sir

Walter Scott were the rage. The local gallants held Ivanhoe-like tournaments, riding horses and spearing rings off trees in honor of their ladies fair. Some of the romantic flavor of these jousts seems to have clung to John Anderson. It was noticeable in his gallantry and swagger. And some of it was wafted his son's way.

"No one," the latter says in his *Memoirs*, "could make remarks about my aunts and mother in my father's presence without getting into serious trouble."

Harry reacted similarly. After he became President, Clare Boothe Luce, wife of the founder of *Time* and *Life*, and Adam Clayton Powell, both then serving in Congress, made unflattering public references to Bess Truman. He barred them from the White House. And when the music critic of *The Washington Post* wrote a barbed review of one of his daughter Margaret's concerts, he struck back with a personal letter to the critic which for uninhibited verbiage is unique in the annals of the presidency.

On being shown a copy of this letter, his appointments secretary, Mathew J. Connelly, said, "My God, you haven't sent this, have you?"

Truman said he had.

"He reached in his desk drawer," Connelly reported, "and he said, 'Here's the first draft.' So I read that. I looked at it and I said, 'All right. I'll settle for the one you mailed.'"

Asked if he meant that the first was hotter than the second, he replied, "Oh, brother!"

The incident compares with one of John Anderson's outbursts. While testifying at a trial, he was asked some questions which he thought improper, so he arose from the witness chair and chased the offending lawyer from the courtroom.

Mize Peters, a boyhood friend of Harry's, remembered tremors of John Anderson's wrath.

"My father was a stockman," he said, "and he had a sales barn right across from the county jail. . . . Harry's father was a stockman, too, and he rode a horse and carried a stub of a buggy whip with him. One day Rube Shrout, a high-tempered, high-strung fellow, came into the barn to get his horse and buggy. He had a knot bleeding on his face, and he was about to cry. My father asked him, 'Rube, what's the matter?' He said, 'I got in an argument with John Truman uptown and he hit me with a whip!'"

It seems likely that John's marriage to Martha Ellen Young did little to abate his touchiness. Her parents, for one thing, were better off than his. Her father, Solomon Young, a trader, stockman, farmer, speculator and leader of wagon trains, could have been the model of a glamorous Westerner (he *was* a model for John). And Martha Ellen, besides being Solomon's prettiest and most spirited daughter, surpassed John Anderson in education. She had gone to a Baptist college, where she had concentrated on music and art. Fond of dancing, too, she described herself as "a lightfoot Baptist." All in all, she made the sort of wife almost any husband might have found it hard to keep up with.

While most of Harry's questions about the past were addressed to Ethel Noland, at least one went to Dean Acheson and prompted a notable reply. He knew, he wrote, that his middle initial, S, did not stand for anything (it had been given him in ambiguous tribute to both his grandfathers, Solomon Young and Anderson Shippe Truman), but he wanted to know more. Acheson replied:

Dear Mr. President:

In your letter to me of December 5, 1957, spurred by your incurable (thank God) curiosity, you asked me this question:

"Do you know the word meaning an initial standing in a name but signifying no name itself, as the 'S' in—Harry S Truman?"

You know, and so do I, how to get at a question of this sort. In my youth an advertisement used to say, "Ask the man who owns one." So I asked the two people who might know—and, of course, they were women—Elizabeth Finley, the librarian of Covington & Burling, past-president of the law librarians of the country, and Helen Lally of the Supreme Court library. Their reports are enclosed.

The essence of the matter is that we are blind men, searching in a dark room for a black hat which isn't there. The "S" in Harry S Truman (no period after "S") does not "stand for anything". Therefore, it cannot have a descriptive noun—"vacuum", "nothing", etc. are already preempted. But, more positively, it *is* something—not representatively but absolutely. You are "S" (without a period) because it is your name.

So, you see, "S" is your middle name, not a symbol, not a letter standing for nothing but an inseparable part of the moniker of one of the best men I have known in a largely misspent life. The same, for that matter, could be said of "Harry".

"Harry" stirs all my deepest loyalties. The senior partner, who brought me up, was christened "J. Harry Covington"; and what a man he was! After years in Congress (he was one of the men who, in 1912 in Baltimore, brought about the nomination of Woodrow Wilson), he had a phrase which to me epitomizes the political obligation, perhaps among the most honorable obligations because resting on honor alone. He never said of an obligation— "I have to do it." He always said, "I have it to do." What a vast difference! In the first, one is coerced into action; in the other, a free man assumes an obligation, freely contracted.

This has a good deal to do with politics—about which you have always thought I knew nothing—in those reaches of it which fit men for government. There are some reaches which unfit them. Honor is a delicate and tricky concept. It does not mean standing by the unfit because of friendship. But it does mean standing by in time of trouble to see a fair deal, when the smart money is taking to the bushes. All of this I learned from the old judge, and relearned again from you in unforgettable days.

So I say that "S" is a good name as it stands, and I am for it. Should either of us have the good fortune to have another grandson, let's agree to persuade his parents to a middle name of just plain "S" with no period, and no explanation.

Indeed, no explanation is possible, because it is the most truly international name. In 1200 B.C. it appeared in the Phoenician as a sort of wobbly "w" but was, unhappily, pronounced *sin*. By 900, in the Cretan, it looked like a 𝟥 and had become *san*, a great improvement. For the next 500 years the 𝟥 was turned around. Then the Latins, Irish, and Saxons, for some odd reason turned it into a "V". Finally the British, as they have so often done, got the thing straight in a wiggle from right to left to right, but not until our colonial ancestors, Ben Franklin included, printed it half the time as an "f" to you and me.

That again is why I like "S" for you. It has had one hell of a tempestuous life. As ever, Dean—

IV

Courting and Farming

THE TRUMANS' RETREAT TO THE GRANDVIEW FARM IN 1906 WAS NOT their first. In 1887, following a couple of John Anderson's failures at cattle trading, they also had found refuge with Martha Ellen's parents. While they were staying there that time, Mary Jane, their last child, had been born and Anderson Shippe Truman had died, leaving his modest estate to his son. When John Anderson decided to invest the inheritance in more cattle trading, Martha Ellen persuaded him to do it in Independence.

> When we moved to Independence in 1890, my mother's first thought was to get us into a good Sunday School. The nearest church to our home to which she was willing to take us was the 1st Presbyterian. So we started to Sunday School there immediately. We went regularly and learned all the good stories of the Old and New Testaments. By the time I was twelve I'd read the whole Book through twice and knew a lot of stories in it which were not particularly stressed in Sunday School—for instance, the final ending of old man Lot's march out of Sodom and David's terrible treatment of Uriah. But the greatest impression I received was the system of morals taught by Moses in the 20th Chapter of Exodus and the Sermon on the Mount as reported in the 5th, 6th, 7th Chapters of the Gospel according to St. Matthew.
>
> We were taught that punishment always followed transgression and my mother saw to it that it did. She kept a good switch and a slipper handy for application to the spot where most good could be accomplished on young anatomy. My father never did punish me except an occasional scolding— which hurt more than a good spanking would have.
>
> When I was eighteen, I joined the Baptist Church and have kept my membership in that Church ever since. My membership now is in the Grand-

view Baptist Church where it has been for forty years. I'm not very much impressed with men who publicly parade their religious beliefs. My old grandfather used to say that when he heard his neighbor pray too loudly in public he always went home and locked his smokehouse. I've always believed that religion is something to live by and not to talk about. I'm a Baptist because I think that sect gives the common man the shortest and most direct approach to God. I've never thought the Almighty is greatly interested in pomp and circumstance, because if He is He wouldn't be interested in "the sparrow" alluded to in St. Matthew's Gospel. Religious stuffed shirts are just as bad or worse than political ones in my opinion.

When my mother started us to Sunday School, she gave us a chance to meet the other children in Independence. I met a very beautiful little lady with lovely blue eyes and the prettiest golden curls I've ever seen. We went through Sunday School, grade school, High School and we're still going along hand in hand. She was my sweetheart and ideal when I was a little boy—and she still is. We have a daughter who "takes after" (that's the way we put it in Missouri) her mother and of course that makes me very happy. (Well, I'm off the beam again).

Along in 1910 we had a very bitter political campaign over the election of an Eastern Judge in Jackson County. After the smoke blew away, my father was appointed road overseer for the south half of Washington township. It was quite a job. He had to fix bridges and culverts, fill up mud holes and try to help everyone in the neighborhood get to and away from his farm in bad weather. There were only a few miles of macadam roads in the township. All the rest were dirt. It was my father's job to collect the poll tax and work it out. A man could work three days on the road or he could pay the road overseer $3.00 and let his road work be done by proxy. One day's work with a team of horses would also give him a clean bill of health. It was my father's policy actually to work the roads for the money. Some of the overseers collected the money and seldom worked. . . .

My father was a very honorable man. If he guaranteed a horse in a horse trade, that guarantee was as good as a bond. If he agreed to do a day's work for a certain amount of money, he'd give good measure on the work. He always expected the people who worked for him to give him a day's work for a day's pay—and woe to a loafer. He made the poll tax workers work for the County just as they worked for themselves. While they'd beef about it on the job, they'd go and brag about how old man Truman gave the taxpayers a fair break. I was taught that the expenditure of public money is a public trust and I have never changed my opinion on that subject. No one ever received any public money, for which I was responsible, unless he gave honest service for it.

When my father passed away in 1915,[1] I was appointed road overseer in his place and served until [the] Presiding Judge became dissatisfied because

[1] John Anderson Truman in fact died in 1914.

I gave the county too much for the money.[2] In the meantime Congressman Borland appointed me Postmaster at Grandview. I let a widow woman, who was helping to raise and educate her younger sisters and brothers, run the office as assistant postmaster and take the pay, which amounted to about $50.00 a month—a lot of money in those days. It would have paid two farm hands.

Although only twenty miles from wide-open Kansas City, Independence might have been in a different country. It was the Athens of the area, noted for its schools and old-fashioned Southern gentility.

And there, in Independence, Harry began both his education and his romance with Bess Wallace. It's doubtful, though, that she was aware of the latter, because he let another five years go by before working up nerve enough to speak to her. Then, he recalled, "It was a big day when she let me carry her books."

Bess Wallace belonged to the town's elite. Her maternal grandfather, George Gates, ran a milling company whose Queen of the Pantry flour was known throughout the Midwest. Her father, although no great shakes financially (he was a minor government bureaucrat), cut a figure with his looks and charm.

Bess's own position was doubly privileged, for she was the only girl among the four Wallace children. As such, you might picture her as spoiled or ultra girlish, but you'd be wrong. According to Henry Chiles (who as a boy had been so impressed with Harry's knowledge):

"They [the Wallaces] lived right next to the Paxtons. The Paxtons were all boys. They were about equal in number and they would get into a big row, the Paxton boys and the Wallace boys, then they'd send Bess in there to settle it. They were all afraid of her. She didn't fool around with them.

"She was the first girl I ever knew who could whistle through her teeth. She could do a good job of it. The boys used to whistle through their teeth, you know, and it would make a real shrill sound. She could do that. When she was growing up, she played ball—anything a boy could do, she could do a little better. You'd think she was a tomboy, but when she was grown, she was the most gracious Southern lady you ever met, as demure as anybody can be. Her mother was a typical Southern lady and Bess was the same way."

Harry's Latin and math teacher, Mrs. Palmer, also taught Bess.

"She would come in," she said, "her desk was right in front of me when I taught that last year at the new high school. I can remember her walking in—her books were strapped in one of those little straps—and she would

---

[2] What he gave the judge was too many suggestions about what ought to be done to the roads. Later, he put some of the ideas to work.

put them down and take her seat and look at you as if to say, 'Well, there they are. . . .'"

"But she was always wonderful—and very interested in sports, just the very thing that Harry couldn't be in, Bess was. I understand she would go anywhere to get into a game of tennis. . . .'"

She and Harry did find common ground in one sport, which Ethel Noland tells about:

"Harry came by every day, and of course Bess was in high school, and they would come here to study—both of them—because part of the time the Wallace family lived in the house on Delaware, beyond Waldo, and part of the time they lived here with the Gateses"—at 219 North Delaware —"because the Gateses were getting older and the house was large and they liked to have Mrs. Wallace live there with them.

"And so, they were at the Gates place a very great deal, and Bess was over here a good deal. So, when it came to Latin, my sister was very good at it and they would come over here to read their Latin with Nellie. I don't know whether they got much Latin read or not because there was a lot of fun going on, and Harry had become interested in fencing. He had two foils or rapiers or whatever you call them; and so we would sometimes practise fencing, which we knew absolutely nothing about, but it was fun to try, and we had the porch and we had room here to play and have fun generally, which we did, with a little Latin intermingled maybe. Though I'm afraid Caesar had a very slim chance with all that was going on.

"But there was a great deal of comradery about it and Harry always was fun. The cousins always liked him. They might quarrel with each other, but there was always peace where Harry was concerned. He was a great peace-maker surely. We were always just good playmates and good comrades, and Bess was the kind of a girl that the boys liked. They liked to play whatever game she liked to play. Harry wasn't any good at tennis. She was—she was really good. There was a tennis court by Woodland College and whether we played much or not we liked to go out there and congregate, you know. Other young people were there. Then there were lots of picnics. The Wallaces had a horse and we could drive and go.

"To tell the truth," she added, "there never was but one girl in the world for Harry Truman from the first time he saw her at the Presbyterian kindergarten. . . . If he hadn't married Bess, he never would have married at all. He would have been like Mr. Harrison Young, a bachelor, I'm sure. . . .'"

Did Bess have other beaux?

"Yes, she had. She was a very popular girl, because she was a good comrade. Some of them liked her just because they loved to be with her and skate or play tennis or do whatever things she enjoyed. But others were very much in love with her. I don't know that she favored any of them particularly. They were glad to go there on any terms that she would let them come, because she was a person that everybody liked to be with. . . ."

"I wouldn't say that I was her beau," Mize Peters said, "but I've taken her to dances. In those days there was a three-story building on the south side of the Square where Penney's is now. On the third floor there was a big ballroom where Miss Dunlap ran a dancing school. We went to the dancing school and had dances there. Sometimes some of us boys would hire an orchestra. We had a time raising the money but we managed to now and then. The girls would bring their dancing slippers in a slipper bag and then put them on after they got there. They couldn't walk in them, because usually we walked to the dance. If we felt right flush and the weather was bad, we'd hire an enclosed cab for a dollar and a half both ways. It was hard to raise the dollar and a half so we didn't do that very often. . . ."

With the move into Kansas City, after his graduation from high school in 1901 and the collapse of his father's final try at cattle trading, Harry's courtship came on lean days. Apparently he saw nothing at all of Bess while he was working in the city (although she was there too, at a finishing school, shot-putting and playing basketball) or later during his first years back on the farm.

They came together again, Ethel Noland says, around 1910. Harry one day was visiting his Noland cousins when he heard that Mrs. Wallace had sent over a cake and that the plate had to be returned. He did the returning. Bess came to the door, and they began again where they had left off.

In the interval, she had experienced a tragedy. A victim of mounting debts and the furies that can hound a man whom life has promised more than it has given, her father had committed suicide. Afterward, just as the Trumans in their trouble had returned to the Grandview farm, Bess, her mother and her brothers had gone to live with her grandparents in the big house on North Delaware Street, across from the Nolands.

In tracing the leisurely progress of Harry's romance, Ethel Noland has been at pains to correct what she considers to be inaccuracies. For example, the character most Truman biographers have given Bess's mother. Mrs. Wallace has been pictured as a kind of cross Truman had to bear throughout his political life; even his severest critics usually give him good marks for his uncomplaining treatment of her.

From her perch at the top of the Independence social heap, she looked down on him, it's said, as on a peasant. Whether he happened to be Judge or Senator or Vice-President or even President, he remained for her the dirt farmer her daughter had stooped to marry. In the crucial 1948 presidential election, for instance, she is reported to have favored the Republicans and, when Dewey lost, thought it a miscarriage of justice. Even in dying she managed what looked like a last slap at her son-in-law. Instead of leaving the North Delaware Street house to Bess and Harry, who had put her up (or put up with her) all their married life, she left it to her children. In order to own it, Harry had to buy out the other heirs.

And yet Ethel Noland says: "She liked him. Mrs. Wallace always liked him; she favored the match from the very start. In fact, we weren't sure whether she liked him better than Bess did or not. But she approved of him because she knew that he had qualities that any girl could bank on in the long run."

As for their all living together, she maintains that they simply wouldn't have done it if there had been any friction. Nor in her opinion did Harry, while courting, extend himself to make an impression on his prospective bride and mother-in-law. The fancy secondhand Stafford car he bought at that time, she says, was not for show but simply for transportation to and from the farm.

"He wasn't a person to put up a good front, you might say. He was a person 'if you like me now you like me and here I am and this is the way I am. You either take me this way or you don't.' In fact the whole family was that way."

And finally she attacks the theory, or implication, that it took the United States entry into World War I to prod the dilatory lovers into getting engaged. They did so, Ethel says, in response to their own impulses, before Wilson's declaration of war.

But with all that set straight, there remains if not a myth a mystery. In later years it was evident to nearly everyone who knew the Trumans that they were devoted to each other. And there seems to be no reason to doubt that the facts were as he gave them, viz.: that he fell in love with Bess on sight, made up his mind to marry her, finally did and lived happily with her ever after.

Still to be explained, though, is the casual way in which he pressed his suit. The pace of his romance makes that at which the average hero and heroine of a long Victorian novel approach their last-page embrace seem downright headlong. Apparently it even puzzled their daughter a little, for in her biography of her father the most enlightening thing she manages to say about his courtship is that it succeeded at last because of his refusal to argue with her mother.

Maybe the moral of the case, if it has a moral, is that the girl to marry is not the one who sends you reeling to the heights or depths but the one you just have fun with.

Well, I went to the farm in 1906 and stayed there contrary to all prophecies until April 1917, really until Aug. 5, 1917. It was a great experience. Wish I'd kept a diary. It was my job to help my father and brother feed the live stock, sometimes milk a couple of cows, then help my mother get breakfast. After breakfast we'd go to the fields. In spring and fall there'd be plowing to do. We had gang plows made by the Emerson Plow Company—two twelve inch plows on a three-wheeled frame. It required four horses or mules to pull it and if an early start was had about five acres could be broken up in a day—not an eight hour one but in say ten or twelve hours. In the spring when the weather was cool and the teams could be kept moving the time was shorter. That sort of plow is the best demonstration of horse power—pounds, feet, minutes. Sometimes the horses gave out and then the power was off until a rest was had.

Riding one of those plows all day, day after day, gives one time to think. I've settled all the ills of mankind in one way and another while riding along seeing that each animal pulled his part of the load. Sometimes in the early part of the year it would be so cold that walking was in order to keep warm, even when a sweater, two coats and an overcoat were worn.

It was always my job to plant the corn, sow the wheat and run the binder to cut the wheat and oats. I usually pitched hay up to my father on the stack also. My father hated a crooked corn row or a skipped place in a wheat field. We had no crooked rows and our wheat and oat fields had no bare places in them and when the binder had finished a wheat or oat field there were no uncut strips in the field. We used a rotation system in our farm program. We'd plant corn after clover. Starting with wheat, we'd sow clover on the wheat field in the spring and usually get a crop of clover hay that fall. The next year we'd spread all the manure from the farm and the little town adjoining it on the clover field. Nearly every family in the little town of 300 people had a cow or two and a horse. My father and I bought a manure spreader and kept it busy all the time when we were not doing other necessary things. We'd break the clover field up in the fall and plant corn the next spring, sow oats in the corn stubble the next spring and wheat after oats. It would take five years to make the complete rotation but it worked most successfully. We increased the wheat yield from thirteen to nineteen bushels, the oats from eight to fifty bushels and the corn from 35 to seventy bushels an acre. Besides these increased yields in the grain crops, we always had two excellent hay crops and at least one seed crop from the clover. So my practical education in farm management took place in those ten years.

In February 1909 I put in an application for membership in Belton Lodge 450 A.F. & A.M. They voted me in and I took the first degree in February, and in March finished up the 3rd. That spring and summer I spent teaching the plow horses all the Masonic lectures. I also found that by counting the number of turns my land wheel made on the gang plow I could measure the acreage of the field I was plowing. So every night there was an accurate check on the amount plowed.

I became very much interested in the work of the Masons and put a great deal of time on it so that in December 1909 I was elected Junior Warden of Belton Lodge. Along in the summer of 1909 it was suggested that Grandview should have a lodge of its own. So after finding that it would require a certain number to start a lodge in Grandview, some of us went to work on it, and in the summer of 1910 succeeded in obtaining enough signers to start out a Lodge Under Dispensation. When the Grand Lodge met in the fall of 1910 a charter was authorized. They made me the presiding officer under dispensation and then elected me in December to serve as first Master under the new charter. The organization has been very successful and a power for good in the community since that date.

In 1924 the Grand Master of the State appointed me his deputy for the 59th District. In 1930 the Hon. William R. Gentry, Grand Master at that time, started me in the Grand Lodge line by appointment and in 1940 the Grand Lodge session in St. Louis on the last Tuesday in September elected me Grand Master. It is a high honor and one for which I am most grateful to my friends and brothers. . . .

A man named Gaylon Babcock has commented on Truman's Grandview days. For a number of years his father had a farm next to the Trumans' and served as a sort of amateur banker, lending money to the neighbors. Babcock's reminiscences stand out from the others on file in the Truman Library because of their tone, which is critical, and their homely details of farm life.

The tone is influenced by his belief that Harry owed him two hundred dollars. Harry didn't think so and made no payment, although at about the same time he was acquiring an almost legendary reputation as a faithful payer of debts. Babcock Senior, it appears, had advanced the two hundred dollars to a bartender named Brauner, and John Anderson Truman allegedly had co-signed the loan. A record of the transaction was discovered after Babcock Senior's death, by which time John Anderson also had died and the bartender long ago had disappeared.

"Mr. J. A. Truman was a very likable man," says Babcock Junior. "Now, as against that, I think Harry's mother's disposition was rather short and caustic; and I can see in his remarks his mother's influence. . . .

"Harry looked after many things around when they were farming for themselves at their farm. . . . Harry's mother did not help in the dining room or kitchen when I was there being served at dinner. Harry and Mary, Harry's sister, invariably waited on the table for us when we were there as harvest help.

"For some reason we were never in their home as a young crowd. I do not know why. Now, they were at our house many times. I had three sisters and we had many parties and a lot of activity in our home; and frankly, Mary, if she ever had a boy friend, I never knew of it, never. And she's single to this day.

"It wasn't because she was not attractive enough. You know, some girls are just so doggone fine, that for some reason or other boys stand aloof. . . . I don't know. If Harry ever had any sweethearts other than the woman he married, I never knew it. Because, you see, his wife lived in Independence; at that time it was quite a distance from where we lived and where Harry lived, and I expect most of his courtship no doubt was over in that area.

"He seemed to be more interested in National Guard work and in reading, and in music. When we were exchanging work at his home, if we had a little time prior to the serving of the meal, instead of coming out and associating with us men, who were waiting for a short time before we ate, he played the piano. It was very noticeable. Mr. Truman and Vivian, who were just the opposite disposition from Harry, seemed to have different interests."

There was another thing Babcock found odd about Harry: he called his mother Mamma. How many men did that? He should have called her Mother, Babcock thought, like everybody else.

"The last day I worked with him, he was on a bundle wagon, but that wasn't ordinarily his work. In fact, he had no set place to work, I mean, he may be doing that job one day and maybe something else another day. . . . I'm not trying to belittle the man. In fact that's somewhat of a compliment, you know, to be able to fill in in different things. . . ."

V

Marriage, Business, Politics

After my discharge [from the Army] I went back to the farm and on June 22, 1919 my wedding to Miss Bess Wallace took place—the same beautiful blue-eyed girl referred to earlier in this manuscript. . . .

"IT WAS A RATHER HOT DAY," ETHEL NOLAND SAID, "AND I REMEMBER that Ted Marks, the best man, had made Harry's suit—Ted Marks being a tailor. I remember when Harry came out of the vestry room as bridegrooms do and stood waiting for the bride how eager and expectant he looked watching for her to come in, and finally here came the wedding march and she was coming in. There were two bridesmaids, Helen Wallace and Louise Wells, a cousin on Bess's mother's side. They had decorated the church in garden flowers. Now, being such a hot day, the garden flowers had drooped a little before the wedding, but nevertheless it was a beautiful wedding.

"Bess didn't wear a veil. She had on a very becoming picture hat, and looked very pretty indeed, and he looked fine and handsome in the tailor-made suit, and they were on their way soon, on the wedding journey. They went to Michigan for one place among several different places. . . . And when they came back from the wedding trip, Harry was determined to live on the Truman farm because he thought he always would be a farmer, but they thought—well, they would stay here for a while before they went to the farm to live. I remember two women that I heard talking about Bess when she came back to Kansas City after they went to the White House, and one of them said, 'Well she doesn't look like she spent her life on a farm, does she?'

"And I would like to have said, 'Well, she didn't.' She never did live on the farm. But it just turned out that this seemed to be the best thing to do—to stay here. . . ."

A native of England, where he had learned the tailor's trade from his father, Ted Marks had emigrated to this country and set up in business in Kansas City. Since he knew a bit about soldiering, having served a hitch in the British army, one of his customers suggested that he join the National Guard. So he went out to the camp, was referred to a clerk and said he wanted to enlist.

"How long have you been in this country?" the clerk asked.

"About six months."

The clerk said, "You speak pretty good English for the time you've been here."

The clerk was Harry Truman.

During the war, the two were assigned to different batteries and saw little of each other. Afterward, they became good friends, and Truman asked Marks to be his best man. Marks joked about it, saying it was just Truman's way of getting a free suit. He made similar suits, of small black-and-white checks, for both of them, and the groom got married in his.

"After the wedding," Marks recalled, "I took his mother down to see Harry off. She had me by the arm, you know, and was a small woman, and I said to her, 'Well, now, Mrs. Truman, you've lost Harry.' And she looked at me with those little blue eyes and said, 'Indeed, I haven't.' And she never did."

> The farm in the meantime had been broken up. My maternal grandmother had left it to my Uncle for whom I was named and my mother. The Uncle lived with us until he passed away, which happened while I was away at war. He left his part of [the] farm to be divided into four parts, one to my mother and the other three parts to my brother, my sister and myself.
>
> When my grandmother died there was a will contest and a settlement, which placed a back-breaking mortgage of about $30,000.00 on the farm. When my Uncle died and the property was divided my mother's part still had to carry a very large part of this mortgage. Accumulated interest and other difficulties had by 1934 increased the charge to about $35,000.00. Although I'd sold some of the land, which my mother and I held together and had paid some ten or fifteen thousand dollars on the indebtedness, it still continued to pile up. Very bad years both wet and dry added to the difficulty so that interest and overhead kept the debt right around $35,000.00.

My canteen sergeant, being a furnishing goods man, wanted to open a store on 12th Street in Kansas City, so I established a line of credit with a couple of banks and we opened a men's furnishing store at 104 West 12th Street along late in 1919. A flourishing business was carried on for about a year and a half and then came the squeeze of 1921. Jacobson and I went to bed one night with a $35,000.00 inventory and awoke next day with a twenty-five thousand dollar shrinkage. . . . All the bank notes were paid off and the merchandise bills were settled as equitably as could be managed. It took several years to clean everything up.

When his postwar traveling-salesman job permitted, Eddie McKim liked to hang out at the haberdashery on Twelfth Street. The store stayed open until 9 or 10 P.M.; it was a sort of clubhouse for Battery D and war veterans in general, ideally situated among the city's saloons and other recreational facilities.

"It was a good haberdashery," said McKim, "and they sold good merchandise, but the depression of the twenties came along and caught them with high-priced merchandise on hand and it wasn't worth what they paid for it. . . . Truman paid back every cent, and I think he paid back what Eddie Jacobson owed, too. . . .

"I liked Eddie very much and admired him. He was always a happy-go-lucky individual. Eddie and a fellow named Francis Barry of F Battery ran a little blind pig—a bootleg joint—on the front line one time. They found a case of tomatoes somebody had snitched off a fourgon wagon and they set up a blind pig in a dugout and traded the tomatoes to the Frenchmen, who loved tomatoes, for a lot of wine and cognac. Business was so good that Eddie and Frank stopped proceedings for a while, watered the stock and then opened up again."

The store was finally closed up along in the latter part of 1922. Early in March 1922 the Democrats began talking about candidates for County Judge for the Eastern District of Jackson County. The Eastern District is all that part of the county outside the city limits of Kansas City.

I had sold my stock and farm equipment early in 1921 and used the money in trying to meet the situation at the store. My wife and I had been living in Independence with her mother. Mr. Wm. Southern, editor and publisher of the Independence Examiner—the most widely read paper outside Kansas City—suggested to some of the Eastern Jackson County politicians that if they wanted a candidate for Eastern Judge who could win they should take an ex-soldier of the late war. He suggested Harry Truman. I knew nothing of this until a delegation of men from the country [sic] came into my store on 12th Street and asked me to run.

My father having been road overseer and both of us having always been interested in politics to some extent, I knew all the men in the delegation personally. They told me about Mr. Southern's suggestion to the "Goat" faction of the Democrats and urged me to go. The Democrats in Eastern Jackson County had always to some extent been alligned [sic] with the two factions in Kansas City. The "Goats" were with the Pendergast faction and the "Rabbits" were with Shannon. . . .

Well, the store was closing up. I liked the political game and I knew personally half the people in Eastern Jackson County. I also had kinfolks in nearly every precinct and I decided to make the race. It was a lot of fun. I opened my campaign in Lee's Summit with Colonel (now Major General) E. M. Stayton making the principal address. The Colonel had been in command of the 110th Engineers in the 35th Division. He knew my war record, what there was of it, and he made the most of it. From June 1 to Aug. 5, 1922 I made every township and precinct in the County, and when the votes were counted on the first Tuesday in August I had a plurality of 500 votes.

The election in the fall went off without incident because Eastern Jackson County is as Democratic as Mississippi or South Carolina. I was sworn in on Jan. 1, 1923 and went to work trying to learn everything I could about the law and the duties attached to my new job. I had an old Dodge roadster, the roughest riding car ever built, but sturdy enough to take the gullies and mud holes of every crossroads in the county. Every road, bridge, lane and every county institution was thoroughly examined. County Court proceedure [sic] was studied in every detail. All this was useful some years afterward. . . .

However charming their wedding may have been, the Trumans got off to a bumpy start. In their mid-thirties, they had no home of their own, and Harry's financial condition was deplorable. He had put up his interest in the heavily mortgaged family farm for the cash he needed for the haberdashery, and now the haberdashery had failed. Yet, despite what his wife, mother-in-law and others may have had had to say about it, he refused to seek refuge in bankruptcy. Eddie Jacobson at first took a similar stand and then weakened. Later, when able to, he paid back his share. But for a while Harry was carrying the full burden of their debt.

Nor was his next decision—to try politics—likely to ease family strains, for at that time and place politics was a career seldom pursued by the people Bess and Mrs. Wallace were used to associating with.

Kansas City and its environs, although largely Democratic, had a vigorous Republican minority which had a way of edging into power when the Democrats were fighting each other, as they often were. At Truman's debut, two major Democratic factions were active, the so-called Goats, under the Pendergasts, and the Rabbits, under the Pendergasts' arch-rival, Joseph Shannon (the nicknames are said to have been bestowed by a reporter, describing the Pendergast custom of herding everybody and everything to the polls, even goats if available, just as Shannon did his Rabbits).

Truman was sponsored not only by Mr. Southern but also by his wartime friend Jim Pendergast and Jim's father, Mike, who was Boss Tom's brother. Among the officials to be elected were the three judges of the Jackson County Court, one for the eastern district, one for the western, and the presiding judge, who represented the county at large. The two former served two-year terms, the last a four-year term. All three were not judges in the usual sense but administrators or commissioners, who levied taxes and cared for roads and county buildings.

Unknown to Truman, who had his eye on the eastern judgeship, Boss Tom had secretly offered that post to the Rabbits, in exchange for their promise to let his man, Henry McElroy, have the western one. The choice of presiding judge was to be charitably left up to the voters. This offstage deal complicated things a bit, as did the emergence of the Ku Klux Klan as a political power.

Later a man named Spencer Salisbury claimed that Truman, a onetime friend with whom he'd had a falling out, had joined the Klan for political reasons. Truman and others declared more credibly that he had rebuffed the Klan on discovering that it would expect him to boycott Catholics and Jews; in short, a lot of his friends and supporters.

In the election after this one—the even more heated election of 1924 the question of his Klan membership was settled to most people's satisfaction, although the press kept reviving it. Hearing that Klansmen had threatened his life, Truman went alone to one of their open, unsheeted meetings, got up and told them what he thought of them. He walked away, untouched, just in time to head off a contingent of his followers, who were coming to his rescue with shotguns.

Anyhow, in the 1922 election he was cast in the role of sacrificial Goat. Tom Pendergast, who had done the casting, either did not notify his brother and nephew of the deal he had made, or perhaps he did and advised them, in a phrase he often used with royal effect, to "let the river take its course."

The river did that, and Truman won. As a consequence, Joe Shannon felt that he'd been double-crossed. He swore to get even and renewed the vow with fervor when the two newly seated Goat judges, Truman and McElroy, outvoting his own presiding Rabbit judge, cornered the rich county patronage. Incidentally, Truman, a stickler for political morality, considered patronage to be the legitimate spoils of the victor. That was the common view of the time, the reason for being of political machines, many of which at the start were less the gang models they later became than quasi-welfare agencies, distributing jobs, food and other favors in return for votes.

* * *

Eddie McKim was traveling during most of Truman's campaign. But he did take part in one of its episodes:

"There was a fellow named Clarence England ran a garage about Fourteenth and McGee Street. I think Clarence had been a flyer in World War I. Anyway, he had one of those old Jennie planes that was held together with baling wire, and at Truman's suggestion, I made a deal with Clarence to take Truman up and drop some leaflets over a picnic at Oak Grove, Missouri. Well, we got them started off and got the leaflets loaded in, took off from the pasture, and circled around this picnic at Oak Grove. Then they were to come down in a pasture right next to the picnic grounds. They came down all right but Clarence had a little trouble stopping the plane and it ended up about three feet from a barbed-wire fence. Our candidate got out and draped himself over this barbed-wire fence and gave forth with a lot of things I know he didn't eat. He was as green as grass. I think it was his first flight, but he mounted the rostrum and made a speech."

Asked what he thought of Truman's speaking ability, McKim replied, "I didn't think he had any. He was a very poor speaker, but he developed."

Colonel Rufus Burrus remembers Truman in his county court days. Senior member of an Independence law firm founded by his grandfather in 1869, the Colonel, a reserve officer, handles a good deal of Truman legal work, Bess's, Mary Jane's, Harry's estate, and some of Vivian's family's, too. I had met him in 1953 and went to see him again in the fall of 1977.

You climb a flight of bare wooden stairs and there in gold letters on the glass upper part of a wooden door is the legend Burrus, Burrus & Gough. A couple of secretaries and their filing cabinets are on view as you enter. The Colonel is in a room to the right, overlooking the street. He sits behind a big desk covered with papers and knickknacks. All around on the walls are framed photographs, mostly commemorating various Trumans and important moments in his own military career. Seventy-seven years old, baldish, fair and nattily turned out in a tweed suit, he has a pink bespectacled face that radiates health and cheer.

When I inquired about the relationship between Truman and Tom Pendergast, he beamed, as though I couldn't have hit on a happier question.

"In the first place, he was running for the eastern judgeship on his own and because some of his own folks asked him to run. And when he was in the contest another battery officer of the 129th Field Artillery, Jim Pendergast, came to him and said, 'Harry, I'd like to take you down and introduce you to Uncle Tom, see if we can't get some support for you.'

" 'I'd like to get all the support I can,' he said, 'but I don't want to be beholden to anybody.'

" 'You don't have to be beholden to anybody. You just come down, he's looking for somebody to make a good candidate to help win, and you're the kind of fella that can help win.'

"So he took him down to see Tom, introduced him to him, and Mr. Pendergast said, 'I understand you want to be eastern judge in Jackson County.'

"He said, 'Yes, I'm going for it.'

" 'Well,' he said, 'I'd be glad to support you.'

"Mr. Truman said, 'I'm pleased about that, but I just want to know what the terms are.'

"Pendergast said, 'All you've got to do is be the Democrat I know you must be or people wouldn't be vouching for you. And you're going to appoint Democrats, I expect, like we've been doing in the past, and I expect you'll appoint friendly Democrats, but you'll choose the friends you want. I'm not going to ask you to appoint anybody.'

"He—Truman—said, 'I made no commitment to him. He never asked me, he never at any time asked me to do anything about appointing anybody. I sometimes would ask him about people who were seeking to be nominated or to be approved, I wanted to be sure they were agreeable to him—' "

"How do you explain Pendergast's attitude?"

"Because Truman was a vote getter," said Colonel Burrus. "He was a man of friendliness, and he impressed not only Tom but other people as having the ability to be a good public official. And Tom realized he needed that more than he needed somebody to do his bidding. He had too many that *would* do his bidding, and it later turned out that he had to go to the penitentiary because they thought that it would be to his glory and their glory to go out and steal the election. And Mr. Truman would have no part of that, didn't have any part of it. . . ."

It was during the 1922 campaign that the Colonel first met Truman.

"I was down here at the bank on the northwest corner of the square, and I was going into the building. He was coming down with Frank Wallace. Frank Wallace was his brother-in-law—he was a ward heeler and I was a precinct worker and had been for some years. He said, 'Rufe, come here, I want you to meet my brother-in-law, Harry Truman.' He said, 'He's going to be the next eastern judge of Jackson County.' I said, 'Mr. Truman, I'm sure glad to know you, glad to know you're Frank's brother-in-law.' And I said, 'Remember, when Frank tells you you're going to be the next judge, you will be, because Frank's always right politically, he always picks the winner.' He smiled and laughed and we talked for a few minutes on the steps.

"Several years after that, after his brother-in-law, Frank, died, I was at the house on account of the death. I said, 'Mr. Truman, I think you probably remember the time that Frank had the occasion of introducing me to you.' He says, 'I sure do. He told you that I was going to be elected eastern judge and you said that I would be because Frank was always right.'

"Now that's the kind of memory the man had. Now that's something that just isn't easy for a fellow to have. He could look at a page and he would know what was on it, and he could recall it when he needed it. He knew how to catalogue it, the names and people's faces, what they had done and who they were. He never had trouble remembering those things."

> The new court was made up of a fine old gentleman by the name of Elihu Hayes, who was the Presiding Judge, and H. F. McElroy, who was judge for the Western District or Kansas City. Judge McElroy had a newspaper complex. He was very friendly to the Kansas City Star and was known as the Star's man on the Court. He also was a close friend of T. J. Pendergast. In fact, he introduced me to T. J. Pendergast, the first time I ever saw him.[1]
>
> The court was almost always in a fuss about something. Hayes representing the "Rabbits" wanted certain jobs in county institutions and as road overseers, and McElroy wanted usually the same jobs for the "Goats". Public service was a secondary matter if the political factions could get the jobs they wanted. I acted as a sort of an arbiter and finally got Hayes, McElroy, Tom and Joe [2] to sit down and reach an agreement so we could get the jobs out of the way and do a little work for the taxpayers. It was an uphill job. By 1924 the factions were so widely split that McElroy and I were beaten for reelection. During 1925 and the early part of 1926, I put on a whirlwind membership campaign for the Kansas City Automobile Club and made a good living at it. . . .

The party split widened because, even after the powwow, the patronage all somehow kept going to the Goats. In 1924, Shannon got his revenge, but at the ruinous price of swinging the election to the Republicans.

And so, at forty, Truman was out of a job again. Meanwhile, his obligations had increased. He had a daughter now and one, it appeared at first, who was going to need a lot of attention. She was slow in learning to talk, slow in growing hair, and she seemed to attract every germ in the neighborhood.

He put on a whirlwind campaign for the Automobile Club, Truman says, and made a good living at it. The fact is he became a one-man whirlwind, going to law school at night, keeping up with his Masonry and reserve officer duties, founding the Reserve Officers Association, becom-

---

[1] There are a number of different versions of this meeting, several by Truman himself.
[2] Tom Pendergast and Joe Shannon.

With a wary eye Harry Truman watches as his car is being parked. He has just driven the nine and a half miles from Independence, taking about thirty minutes for the regular trip to his Kansas City office. He occupied this office from January 1953 until 1957, when he moved to more spacious quarters in the newly completed Harry S. Truman Library.

Operator of the parking lot is Joe Cavello. Joe expounds on the benefits to be gained if Truman went into the parking lot busi- ness with him. The ex-President is inter- ested, polite—and entirely noncommittal.

▲ In his Kansas City office, Citizen Truman dictates to longtime executive secretary Rose Conway, who also worked with him at the White House. Truman enjoyed writing letters as much as dictating them, and he almost always added a handwritten personal message.

▼ Truman's office in the Federal Reserve Bank Building was like the office of a busy doctor. There was always a steady stream of visitors—some old friends, many slight acquaintances, but mostly strangers who wanted to see (and ask a favor of) the ex-President. Frances Myers kept the outer office orderly and gave everyone a fair chance.

▲ Clang, clang went the burglar alarm as Truman inadvertently set it off while attempting to open the door to the room in the basement of the Courthouse where his presidential papers were stored. "There is nothing to do now but wait to be arrested," joked Truman.

▶

The local police officer and building security guard were quickly on the scene with forms to be signed and a new instruction sheet for the confused ex-President. "It was my second offense," he said. "I can't afford to do it again."

This was the temporary repository of the Truman presidential papers. They were consulted regularly by Citizen Truman, especially when writing his *Memoirs* and, in 1953, *Mr. Citizen.* Later they were moved into the Truman Library and now form an important part of its reference section. Truman thus made available to all scholars, teachers and historians valuable source material for the study of the history of the United States.

Even in a large town like Kansas City, Truman could not walk down the street without being stopped at least once. Here, on his way to the barber, the ex-President is stopped by two waitresses. Object: autographs.

As well as being careful about his sartorial image, Truman was very particular about his haircut. Barber Frank Spina was Truman's favorite haircutter. He was, in addition, a very old friend who had served under Captain Truman in World War I. Frank gave Truman just the kind of trim he wanted. "I remember when he gave Margaret her first haircut." Besides, Truman said, he greatly enjoyed the relaxing half hour he spent in the chair. He also had a good word for Bob, porter and shoeshine expert.

▶

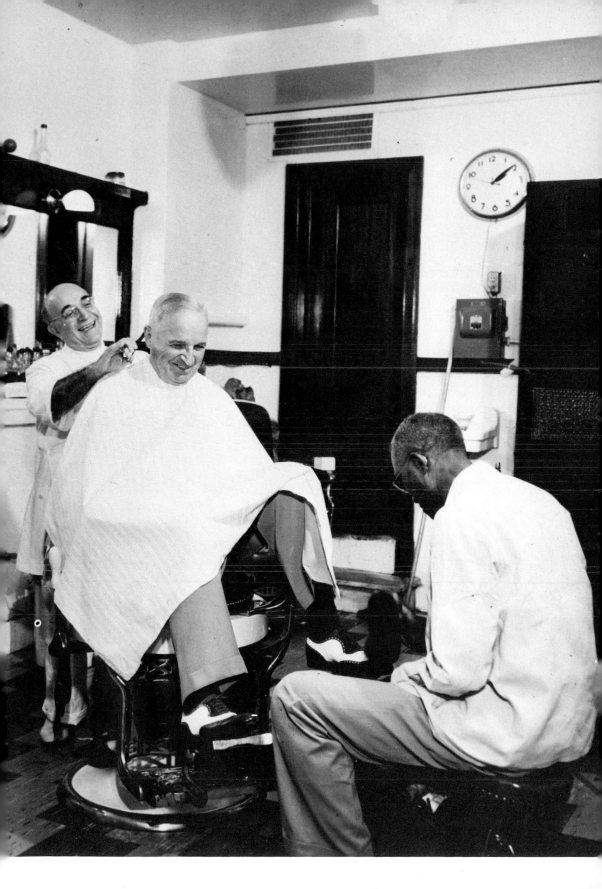

Another day and another morning drive from Independence to the Kansas City office in the Federal Reserve Bank Building. The summer heat never seemed to bother Truman. Even when the thermometer hit 101°—not unusual in the Midwest—he would wear his usual dress shirt, tie and suit.

Truman preferred face-to-face contact but often used the telephone as the next best thing. In addition to making calls about business and favors for friends, either he or Bess Truman called Margaret almost every day—or she called them.

In Kansas City, as in Washington, Truman took a special interest in high school students and took time to meet and talk to them. He hoped to arouse their enthusiasm, especially for the study of world history. Meetings with Future Farmers of America and 4-H Club members he found invigorating and informative. He once remarked that he learned as much from their questions as he did from those asked by journalists at press conferences.

Having lunch at Kansas City's Pickwick Hotel with his staff, the former President was, as usual, besieged by autograph seekers. Here he graciously obliges Mrs. Grace Fantus, a visitor to Kansas City from Chicago, who holds on to her restless child. Truman was never impatient on such occasions. He liked to say that he knew how he would feel if someone "high-hatted" him.

Here are four of Truman's closest and oldest friends:

Monsignor L. Curtis Tiernan was his Army chaplain in Battery D. Most of the soldiers in that artillery unit were Catholic; Captain Harry was one of the few Protestants. But Truman never forgot the priest. Monsignor Tiernan was present to give blessings and prayers at many functions after Truman became President.

Harry Jobes was another Army buddy whom Captain Truman never forgot. Jobes had also been a captain in the 129th Artillery.

Eddie Jacobson and Truman met before the war when Eddie had a job in a clothing store. Both were stationed at Camp Doniphon (Fort Sill, Oklahoma) and Truman gave credit to Jacobson for helping make the canteen, which they ran together, a success and thus getting him promoted to captain. After the war they became partners in Truman and Jacobson haberdashery. The store closed after three years and Truman's political career began.

It was during Truman's 1922 campaign that Rufus Burrus first met Truman; they were introduced by Frank Wallace, Bess Truman's brother. A leading Independence attorney, member of a firm founded by his grandfather in 1869, Burrus was not only Truman's friend but his lawyer, and, upon occasion, his political adviser as well.

Lunch at the Muehlebach "Hideaway" shows, left to right, Truman's "old cronies," Tom Evans (owner of a drugstore chain and radio and TV stations), Monsignor Tiernan, Eddie Jacobson, the ex-President, Harry Jobes, General Ralph Truman (Harry's first cousin), Rufus Burrus, and, back to camera, Vivian Truman (Harry's younger brother). While I was preparing to take the picture, the ex-President said, "Maybe we'd better get all the cocktail and highball and wine glasses off the table first." All were cleared away except those of Tom Evans and Monsignor Tiernan.

ing president of the National Old Trails Association, organizing a Regional Planning Association and getting involved in two sideline businesses with his then friend Spencer Salisbury.

His enrollment in the Kansas City School of Law took place in 1923. After maintaining a B average, he dropped out two years later. So many people, especially the Battery D boys, he explained, were coming to him for help and advice that he couldn't get in the necessary studying.

He had a quality that attracted people. Numerous witnesses have testified to it. Some have maintained that it was more in evidence with men than with women, that he was shy and uneasy in the company of women he didn't know well, but I never noticed anything like that. At their first meeting, my wife and he began talking away as though they'd been acquainted for years; she was charmed with him. "Charm" may be the word for this quality of his. Another word was suggested by Stanley Woodward, whom he later appointed Ambassador to Canada.

"One thing that stuns me: what seemed to be so little recognized," Woodward said, "is his affability. I never could understand why it wasn't understood by more people. I used to think it was because he didn't photograph well, because of his glasses you couldn't get the expression in his eyes. The lenses reflected the light—something. When you took a man in to call on General Marshall or President Roosevelt, for instance, they would come back with their previous impression confirmed rather than altered. It's very interesting that their previous impressions of President Truman were always changed. What the explanation for it is I don't know. I think they were expecting someone much less affable, more dour, more severe and less colorful. They expected someone less responsive."

Truman himself seemed to have a soft spot for men who exhibited a kind of parody of his own charm or affability. They were the fast-talking extroverts, the operators, those whom T. S. Eliot called "the low on whom assurance sits / As a silk hat on a Bradford millionaire." Before World War I there was Jerry Culbertson, who talked him into his first two losing business ventures, a zinc mine and an oil prospecting company. After the war, Culbertson's place was taken by Spencer Salisbury, who also had commanded a battery in the 129th Field Artillery.

In 1926, Salisbury persuaded Truman to go into partnership with himself and another man. The Security State Bank of Englewood, a small town near Independence, was for sale. No cash needed. The three just signed notes for $30,000 and the bank was theirs. After recruiting an impressive board of directors, they discovered that the Security State Bank was just a front which the Republican Secretary of State of Missouri had set up for his own purposes; its chief assets were transient funds from state auto license fees, against which the Secretary would borrow money for his printing business. The three partners unloaded their stock in time to escape getting hurt, but quite a few people weren't so lucky.

Nevertheless, just as he had gone into oil drilling with Culbertson right after drawing a blank at the zinc mine, Truman was soon involved again with Salisbury, this time in a savings and loan association. They did quite well for a while, until they quarreled. According to Truman, Salisbury lined up enough proxy votes to oust him and other directors; then he installed his own people and began manipulating the company.

Salisbury asserted that he was only protecting their going concern from Truman's effort to merge it disadvantageously with a savings and loan run by Jim Pendergast. In any case he got control of the association and from then on was perhaps the outstanding local anti-Trumanite. He conspicuously opposed Truman in successive elections and also contributed his bit to the downfall of Tom Pendergast and the Pendergast machine.

In the late thirties, Salisbury resigned from the savings and loan association and sued it for damages. The suit backfired and he wound up serving a fifteen-month prison sentence. When Truman was President, Father Tiernan, who had been chaplain of the 129th Field Artillery, asked him to grant his former friend and fellow veteran a federal pardon, but Truman refused.

"I don't know if I should say it right out," Eddie McKim remarked of Salisbury, "but in my opinion he's an eighteen-carat crook. We used to call E Battery, which he commanded, 'Carranza and his forty thieves,' that was the nickname of his battery, the captain and his battery. Nobody had any respect for him at all. He came out to reserve camp a couple of times. I knew he used to bring a half pint of whiskey with him and he'd take home a half pint.

"One time he arranged a snipe hunt. He picked on a fellow named Captain Calhoun, who looked like a big yokel, and he was going to take him on a snipe hunt. So Cal told me about it and we framed a deal. We let Calhoun go along and play the part. 'Carranza' and his mob took him out and planted him with the sack, while they were going out to herd the snipes in. In the meantime, Frank Fisher, Cokey Cohagen and myself stole their horses. Carranza was a little mad when they had to walk back from those hills around Fort Riley."

Although McKim would have recoiled from the idea, it seemed to me that he and Harry Vaughan bore a kind of generic resemblance to Culbertson and Salisbury. Colonel Burrus did not agree.

"Harry Vaughan," he said, "was the athletic director of the St. Louis school system. In our regiment, when we had training, Mr. Truman put him in charge of the calisthenics department. In the morning we'd get up —why we'd go out and have calisthenics. Harry was a good storyteller and friend. He was a gentleman, taught a Sunday school class, came from a school around here, a Presbyterian college, and he was the cause of Mr. Truman's obtaining the presence of Churchill when Churchill made the outstanding Iron Curtain speech.[3]

"Well, over the years Vaughan still was at the meetings of these summer camps we'd have at Fort Riley. When Mr. Truman got to be Senator he [Vaughan] helped campaign for him in St. Louis, helped to get money for him from some of the friends in St. Louis, they were all his personal friends. There was nothing raffish about that man, he was one of the finest gentlemen. He gives you the impression with some of the things he says and does that people get—put a wrong slant to it.

"Just now he's been hurt, both of his legs, and he's getting a little vague, they tell me. But Harry was just a gentleman and he could be gracious and voluble. They'd call him sometimes, people would, the court jester. He'd tell you a good story and get things in a light vein. He was the kind of person Mr. Truman needed to get some of the seriousness off of him."

"What about Eddie McKim?"

"Eddie McKim was a noncom in his battery, and he was an Irishman from Kansas City. I met him for the first time—Mr. Truman picked him up over on Genesee Street and took him along with me to Fort Riley in his Dodge roadster in 1926, I think the year was, and we got to know each other. Well, Eddie was just a typical Irishman. But he was a good Catholic, he had a daughter that married a lawyer over in Omaha. He made some money and took care of his mother and got retired on some sort of basis. . . ."

The nineteen twenties were the period when the quadripartite friendship among Truman, McKim, Vaughan and John W. Snyder took shape. Of the last three, Snyder, an Arkansas banker who transplanted himself to St. Louis, became the closest to Truman. Mrs. Truman helped to bring this about. She never warmed up much to McKim and Vaughan. During Truman's presidential days, for instance, McKim either was asked or took it upon himself—accounts differ—to streamline the White House operation. One of his first moves was to fire a bunch of stenographers who were answering the hundreds of letters of condolence Mrs. Roosevelt had received on her husband's death. When Mrs. Truman found out what he'd done, the story went, McKim was exiled to the Treasury Department.

[3] Delivered March 5, 1946, at Vaughan's alma mater, Westminster College, Fulton, Missouri.

I mentioned this to Colonel Burrus, who smiled and said:

"Out of her hair. She knew that Eddie had his place and one of the places was not to be around where she was."

As between Truman and Snyder, on the other hand, the relationship was not just man to man but family to family.

In 1977, with McKim dead and Vaughan in the condition Colonel Burrus described, Snyder, the last to join the four musketeers of Fort Riley, also was the last firsthand source of information about them. Unfortunately the material by and about him in the Truman Library was either sealed (at his request) or of minor interest from my point of view. So I decided to try to see him in Washington, D.C., where he still was active as chairman of the Harry S. Truman Scholarship Foundation. The upshot of the effort appears farther along in these pages.

VI

The Climb

When the politicians met early in 1926 to decide on procedure for the fall campaign, I went to see Mike Pendergast and told him I'd like to run for County Collector. It was a good job at that time and paid a return to the Collector of about $25,000 per year. I figured I could make a record collecting back taxes and could also pay all my accumulated debts and maybe go back to the farm at the end of eight years and enjoy life. Mike Pendergast was young Jim's father who was my personal friend. He was anxious for me to have what I wanted. But it didn't happen.

T.J.[1] and his advisors (and he had a very competent staff of advisors at that time) decided that since I was familiar with the County Court business I'd be a better public servant as Presiding Judge of the County Court. Besides that, an older man and one who had been with the Organization longer was entitled to be County Collector. I filed for Presiding Judge much to the disgust of Mike Pendergast, who wanted me to make a fight for Collector.

There was no opposition in the primary and my majority in the fall election was a little over 16,000 votes. In the spring of 1926 Kansas City adopted a new Charter, which created a City Manager form of government. The Democrats won five of the nine aldermen and they elected Judge McElroy as City Manager. He made an excellent City Manager for more than eight years and then the scandals came and he died just a short time before Tom Pendergast was convicted of income tax evasion.

I set to work as Presiding Judge to clean up the County's financial condition. The number of employees was reduced, the road overseers cut down

---

[1] Tom Pendergast.

from sixty to sixteen, a budget system installed, outstanding county warrants were called in and refinanced on a low interest basis and plans were prepared for a county road and public building program. . . .

In 1928, Kansas City on the advice of a Committee of One Hundred of the leading business men, labor leaders and professional men decided to make a major plan for civic improvements. This plan included a new city hall, civic auditorium, water works plant and traffic entrances to the city. . . . It was my job to try and get the County's bond plan included at the same election at which the city's would be voted upon.

The political leaders did not think a bond issue for the County would carry. . . . I told the politicians . . . that if I could go to the voters and assure them that . . . able engineers and architects would have control of the construction and that no payments would be made by the Court without their approval, I thought the bonds would carry. Pendergast and Shannon told me to tell the voters anything I pleased. I made it perfectly plain to both of them that I intended to carry out the promise if the bonds carried.

The bonds did carry, and the program was carried out to the letter. . . . When the election of 1930 came up we were in the midst of the building and budget reform programs so the Presiding Judge [2] and Associate Judges favorable to the policy being pursued were returned to office. The majority of the Presiding Judge was over 58,000. It was in fact a vote of confidence.

ONE REASON FOR TRUMAN'S WIN IN 1926, AFTER HIS DEFEAT IN 1924, was the new charter he speaks about. Adoption of the charter halted hostilities between the Goats and the Rabbits.

Those who proposed and voted for the charter believed that it would usher in an era of clean government. They were considerably surprised when Tom Pendergast emerged in firmer control of Kansas City than he had been before. In an election that even the opposition press had to admit was honest, his forces captured five of the nine aldermen's seats, and, thanks to this majority, he could name his own City Manager, Henry McElroy. His victory brought about a truce with Joseph Shannon, whom later, in a lordly manner, he kicked upstairs into the United States House of Representatives.

Truman—now at the head of an all-Goat court, with the friendly backing of Mike Pendergast and with Boss Tom preoccupied with grandiose schemes of his own—felt free at last to do something about the projects he'd had in mind since his and his father's days as road overseers. He was going to give Jackson County a course of health and beauty treatments it would not soon forget.

"He took over the county," said Colonel Burrus, "when it had a great debt against it. That came about because there was no way to control the

[2] I.e., Harry Truman.

expenditures of the county through the county court, because the elected officers would incur indebtedness and the county would have to issue warrants to pay for it. He thought the county's credit ought to be good and the only way to control the credit was to control your expenditures. So he went to the legislature and helped to get a budget law through, which provided that the county court set the budget for each one of the different officers, the sheriff, the assessor, the collector and so on."

"That couldn't have made him very popular."

"It didn't. But in time it did, because they didn't have these warrants that were dishonored—"

"I mean among members of the official family."

"I'll give you an illustration of that. A circuit judge, Clarence Burney— It was necessary for the court to curtail expenditures when they were exceeding the limit, so Truman, as presiding judge, just arbitrarily cut off a certain percent of all the pay that all the county officials were getting, including certain judges—not their salary, because that came from state funds—but parole officers, juvenile commissions and other things that went into their salaries but that amounted to about half what they were getting from the state.

"Well, I had a matter before Judge Burney where the question of governmental immunity came up; I claimed that governmental immunity exempted the county from being liable for tort. And in my explanation to the judge I said that governmental immunity goes back to the common law that the King can do no wrong.

" 'Wait a minute, wait a minute! You don't mean that the county can do no wrong, like the King can do no wrong!'

" 'Well, that's the theory of it—'

" 'They sure did wrong to me; they cut my salary!'

"And he didn't say it in jest, he did it in anger.

"Mr. Truman also believed that we should have a road program, to have new roads in the county, because they had what they called 'piecrust' roads that had been built by Miles Bulger and others. Mr. Truman saw the need of having this road program, and he knew he had to sell the people of the county, taxpayers and newspapers and other public people, to be willing to vote bonds, because bonds had to be voted to get the money to do it.

"So he went to Mr. Pendergast and told him what his plan was to get the people to vote for the bonds, and in order to do that he had to have them understand that it was going to be done professionally by professional engineers and [the contracts] would be let to the lowest bidders and they [the roads] would be built according to specifications. . . ."

* * *

Pendergast did not jump at Truman's bond proposal, nor did he flatly reject it. On the whole he was negative, because the county voters had turned down a couple of similar issues in the past, expecting nothing from them but graft. Besides, he had unpleasant memories of his former presiding judge, Miles Bulger, whose malfeasance had been glaring, and, in addition to that, he, with McElroy, was about to float a Kansas City bond issue of his own, a big one, for $28 million, and there was a chance that Truman's on top of his would sink them both.

But Truman was not easily put off. After giving his plans another polishing, he came back to say that they were sure-fire, they were bound to go over, if only he could tell the constituents exactly what he proposed to do. And Pendergast, absorbed in his project, as though brushing aside a fly, now told him to go ahead and do whatever he wanted.

Truman went to the voters. He traveled all over the county, giving people the straight facts. His forty-fourth birthday fell the day after the election, and he woke up that morning to learn that his $6.5 million bond issue had carried, every cent of it, whereas Pendergast's $28 million had been trimmed down to $750,000.

Some weeks later, an unusual scene was enacted in the boss's office. Three Pendergast cronies, all contractors and all unhappy, were there to complain that Truman, who had been summoned to the meeting, was not behaving as a Goat should. Instead of giving them his road business, he was letting the contracts to strangers, some as far away as South Dakota.

Truman replied that he was letting them to the lowest bidders, just as he had told the boss and the voters he was going to do. If these contractors would lower their bids, fine, he'd be glad to consider them. Everyone then looked at Pendergast, who said to his three friends, "I told you he was the contrariest cuss"—or "mule" or "man"; he is variously quoted—"in the state of Missouri." And that was that. The meeting was adjourned, with the defendant unrebuked and unrepentant.

Not the least remarkable part of this affair was the fact that Pendergast was known to be the silent partner of one or more of the complainants. So why did he behave as he did? In suggesting that he was carried away by Truman's independence, some interpreters have given little credit to his cunning, realism and ruthlessness. It seems more likely that, in looking at Truman, what he saw was $6.5 million as against a paltry $750,000. If, he may have thought, the way to get that kind of money was to act the way this guy was acting, well, then, more power to him.

There was a sequel. Although Truman's account above fails to say so, two bond issues were launched by both Jackson County and Kansas City. The meeting with the contractors followed the first. After his reelection as presiding judge in 1930, Truman asked permission to float more bonds to complete his program. This time Pendergast was happy to oblige. He made Jackson County's issue the bellwether of a second whopping one the city was preparing. And, as he apparently had hoped, Truman's reputation for honesty helped to win approval for both issues.

Another noteworthy feature of the contrary judge's performance was a 24,000-mile automobile trip he took in order to inform himself of what other communities across the country were doing about their roads and public buildings. He made the trip at his own expense. He had a way of doing things like that. In Grandview, for instance, one of his new roads sliced off a bit of his mother's farm, and to her indignation he refused to compensate her for the loss.[3]

He did not publicize such oddities or pride himself on them, although, when they were discovered, he took some pleasure in the stir they caused. "It's like old Mark Twain said," he would observe. " 'Always do right. This will gratify some people, and astonish the rest.' "

He liked being presiding judge, but the job had its drawbacks. One was the comparatively low salary—$6,000 a year. Another was the cost to family life of so much work and traveling. In the manner of part-time fathers, he was inclined to spoil his daughter, to the annoyance of his wife. The tendency reached a high point on Margaret's eighth birthday, when, in recognition of her musical aptitude, he presented her with a baby grand piano. She burst into tears, for she had been hoping for an electric train.

But perhaps the most serious of his job's drawbacks was the fact that presiding judges never served more than two terms. So, as his second term drew to a close, Truman, at fifty, was faced once more with the familiar question of what to do next.

In 1934, while traveling for a Nebraska insurance company, Eddie McKim received word that one of the firm's Kansas agents seemed to have absconded with the receipts. On his way to look into the matter, he stopped off in Kansas City and borrowed Truman's car. Then he recalled:

"I said, 'Where can I leave you off?'

"And he said, 'Oh, I'm going with you.'

"So we drove up to Atchison and I looked all around for our man but he'd really gone south. So, driving back we were talking politics and Truman said:

" 'What would you do? Here's the situation. I will have had eight years as county judge and under the system of the Democratic organization that's all I can have there. The only other job, the best paying job in the county,

---

[3] Later, as President, he would stamp and mail his personal letters.

is county collector. I've talked to Tom Pendergast and Tom says that I can have the job for eight years and it pays about $20,000 a year. On the other hand, there is a new congressional district that's right out in my part of the country, and that job pays $10,000 a year. Tom says that if I take that I can have it the rest of my life. Now what would you do?'

"And I said, 'Well, if you took the collector's job at $20,000 a year and you have it just eight years, when you finish you're still a young man and you're through politically. There isn't any other job in the county that you can have. On the other hand, if you take the congressional job, it pays half as much money but you can keep it the rest of your life. You'll be going to Washington; you'll be in the big swim there and nobody can tell what will happen. If I were you, I would take the congressional job.'

" 'Well,' he said, 'you're telling me what I want to hear.'

" 'Well,' I said. 'I don't give a damn what you want to hear. You asked me and I told you.' So I told him then, 'I'm going to file for the Nebraska legislature.'

"He said, 'When are you going to file?'

"And I said, 'By the way, who's going to be the Senator from Missouri?'

"And he said, 'Oh, Jim Aylward. Jim's been a party wheelhorse; he's been state chairman and national committeeman and all, and he's picked to be the Senator.'

"So I guess it was a couple of weeks later or so, I got a long-distance call from Mr. Truman and he said, 'Did you file for the legislature?'

"And I said, 'I sure did.'

" 'Well,' he said, 'I was down at Jeff City today and I filed.'

"I said, 'Good.'

"He said, 'But I filed for the Senate.'

"I said, 'What happened to Jim Aylward?'

" 'Well,' he said, 'Jim has a very lucrative law practice and he felt that he couldn't afford to be a Senator. So Tom told me that if I was so hell-bent on going to Washington to run for the Senate. Jim Pendergast, I think, put the bee in his bonnet. Anyway, I filed for the Senate.'

"So I said, 'Good luck to you.' "

McKim did not take part in Truman's campaign, being busy with his own run for the Legislature. He was elected by fifteen votes. That was his one and only taste of public office. In 1938, he was a candidate for Lieutenant Governor but was defeated. Senator Truman came to Nebraska and made a speech in his behalf, he said and added:

"He thinks it helped defeat me."

In 1932 [Truman's sketch continues] the Kansas City Democratic Organization (Pendergast and Shannon) endorsed Charles M. Howell for

United States Senator. Bennett Champ Clark was the other (Democratic) candidate. When the votes were counted in the August primary that year, Mr. Howell had 110,000 votes in Kansas City and Jackson County and had carried about three other counties. Clark carried all the rest of the State and was overwhelmingly nominated and was elected that fall.

In the spring of 1934, Missouri was now voting on a bond issue to enlarge the various eleemosynary institutions. . . . Governor Park asked me to make some speeches out over the State and help make the bond issue a success. . . .

Along in the first week in May, I was speaking in Warsaw, Missouri, on the bond issue when I received a phone call from Sedalia, which is about 30 miles from Warsaw, asking me to stop at the Bothwell Hotel on my way north and have a talk with Jas. P. Aylward, the State Chairman of the Democratic Committee, and Jim Pendergast, nephew of T.J. and my war buddy.

I stopped and talked to them and they urged me to run for the nomination to the United States Senate. I told them that I had no legislative experience, that I thought I was something of an executive and I'd rather wait two years and run for Governor. But they insisted that I owed it to the party to run, that Sen. Clark was from the eastern side of the State and that Jackson County was entitled to one of the Senators.

Aylward assured me that he could line up his friends in St. Louis and that I've have no trouble beating Tuck Milligan, who was Congressman from the 3rd District and who had been endorsed by Sen. Clark. Well, after some argument back and forth I went to Jefferson City and filed for the Senate.

When President Roosevelt was inaugurated in March 1933, Tom Pendergast was doing nicely. He had a pipeline to the Democratic Governor, Guy B. Park. In Kansas City, Henry McElroy still was his loyal City Manager. Some difficulties had arisen there with organized crime, but he had skillfully enticed its local leader, one Johnny Lazia, into the Pendergast fold and made him a watchdog against outside gangsters.

The only fly in all this ointment was Senator Bennett Clark, son of Champ Clark, former Speaker of the House. After being elected Missouri's Senior Senator in 1932 without Pendergast help, Clark boasted that he was going to make his wartime friend, Congressman Jacob L. (Tuck) Milligan, Junior Senator in the 1934 election. If he should succeed in commanding both Senate seats, along with the rich federal patronage that went with them, there was a chance that he would also make good on his second boast: to smash the Pendergast machine and boss the whole state.

The chance increased in February 1934, when he persuaded Roosevelt to name Tuck Milligan's brother and law partner, Maurice, U.S. Attorney for the western district of Missouri, with special instructions from the

Attorney General to investigate crime in Kansas City. A sensational incident had opened the way for this move. Despite Lazia's watchdogging, a gun battle had broken out in Union Station. Three out-of-town gangsters had tried to free a fourth, who was being taken to the penitentiary; the prisoner, a police chief, an F.B.I. man and two Kansas City policemen had been shot dead.

Maurice Milligan was still ruminating that affair when the Kansas City municipal election of March 1934 gave him something equally juicy to chew on. Pendergast goons went after the fusionist opposition with everything they had, including guns. The vote, when counted, gave the Boss a great victory, the casualties (four dead, eleven wounded), the start of his downfall. He celebrated the former—and speeded the latter—by betting on a long shot at the track. The horse came in and earned him almost a quarter of a million dollars, turning what had been a gambling fever into a galloping mania.

Meanwhile, he was looking for a candidate to run in the Democratic senatorial primary against the redoubtable seven-term Congressman Tuck Milligan. His first choice, retired Senator James Reed, refused, as did his second, Joseph Shannon, and his third, Democratic State Chairman James Aylward. All three thought the odds were too great. And that apparently left Truman.

Why Truman? After being rebuffed three times, Pendergast may have decided to do as he'd done in the horse race and pick a long shot. If he lost by doing so, he at least wouldn't be losing much face, and if he won he might make a killing. Moreover, Truman's track record, although skimpy, was good; and, as Joe Shannon observed, he had the advantage of being "clean."

The cleanliness illuminates a note Truman wrote to himself at the time: "Now I am a candidate for the United States Senate. If the Almighty God decides that I go there, I am going to pray, as King Solomon did, for wisdom to do the job."

Whether or not as a sign that he had been heard, a third candidate presently surfaced. He was John J. Cochran, of St. Louis, an *eight*-term Congressman, with an excellent record and the friendship of the President. Anything, of course, can happen in a three-man race, but Cochran's entry was thought to be more damaging to Milligan than to Truman. Indeed, there was a rumor that Pendergast was so much of that opinion that he had lured Cochran into the contest.

All three candidates favored Roosevelt, so political issues were incidental. The main issue was bossism. Milligan was called Clark's office boy;

Cochran, the office boy of the *St. Louis Post-Dispatch*; and Truman, of Pendergast.

> Mr. Aylward couldn't do any good in St. Louis. The Democratic organization there had a candidate of their own, Congressman John J. Cochran.
> It was a tough three-cornered race. When the smoke blew away, I was nominated by some 40,000 plurality. I got the votes in Jackson County, Cochran got those in St. Louis and St. Louis County and Milligan, Cochran and I split the country vote. . . .
> The election in the fall of 1934 was a pushover for the Democrats. So I came to the United States Senate and went to work. . . .

Beyond pointing out that both his opponents had not been above seeking Pendergast's help in their last campaigns for Congress, Truman did less name-calling than they did. But, even though he was the winner, he was hurt the most. For to be the office boy of Clark or a distinguished newspaper was one thing, of Pendergast, another. The label stuck to Truman long after the election and did nothing to brighten his early years in Washington.

VII

Senator

NOT MANY FRESHMAN SENATORS HAVE ARRIVED IN THE NATION'S CAPITAL feeling more humble than Harry Truman did. He fairly reeked of humbleness. The Senate Democratic whip, J. Hamilton Lewis, of Illinois, caught a whiff of it and told him kindly that it was the usual thing for Senators to wonder at first how they ever managed to get there; then they'd start wondering how the other Senators got there.

And there was Victor Messall, whom Truman had been advised to take on as his administrative assistant. The capital-wise Messall had been secretary to a Missouri Congressman who had lost in the last election. During his interview with Truman, he decided that there was no point in exchanging one loser for another and turned down the offered job. However, he did help to find an apartment and by the time that had been done was feeling so sorry for the new Senator that he agreed to go on helping him.

In Washington, the main stage of the history he'd been reading since childhood, Truman was acutely aware of the political cloud hanging over him and of his personal shortcomings, in particular his lack of formal education, of legislative experience and of money. So once more he resorted to his usual panacea—work. Just as he'd become the studious kid with glasses and all the answers, he now began to build a reputation as the studious Senator, who relished the most boring committee jobs and could quote you statistics on everything from raising peafowl to the population of Timbuktu.

The results were beneficial for him but less so for his wife. Crowded into a four-room apartment, with a preoccupied husband and without the supportive small-town social life she was used to, she couldn't have felt lonelier if she'd *been* in Timbuktu. Margaret, then eleven, at least had her school and homework. Bess's chief activities were sightseeing and telephoning friends in Independence when she felt she could afford it (which wasn't too often, since their only income was Harry's salary of $10,000 a year, and the price of everything in Washington was about twice what it was in Missouri).

Yet, despite all his busyness, Truman remained a dedicated family man. His then secretary, Mildred Dryden, also from Independence, said:

"He would get down there [to the office] early—I suppose he was just about the only Senator there who would be there early. When I walked in, he was either reading the *Congressional Record* or writing a letter to his mother and sister. Now that was every day practically. I remember one time I came in and I said, 'You make me feel ashamed,' because he wrote home so much and I'd probably be owing a letter home."

> I was in luck on Committee assignments [Truman says in his autobiographical sketch], Interstate Commerce, Appropriations and a couple of minor ones. . . . Senator Wheeler [of Montana] was Chairman of Interstate Commerce and Senator Glass [Virginia] was Chairman of Appropriations. Wheeler had succeeded in getting a resolution through the Senate authorizing the Interstate Commerce Committee or any subcommittee thereof to investigate the financial transactions of the Railroads. . . .
>
> Being interested in transportation and communications, I attended the meetings of the subcommittee. Wheeler saw that I was interested and finally made me one of the subcommittee members, and later its vice-chairman. Sitting as a 'hearing committee' is a dull boresome procedure and it requires patience and persistence. So I soon became the 'patient and persistent' member of the subcommittee . . . on RR finance. The work of that subcommittee finally resulted in the Transportation Act of 1940—the Wheeler-Truman Bill.

One of his first-term speeches, and a notable one, was on the subject of railroads. He likened the railroad barons to Jesse James and his gang in all but the amount of their loot, which made Jesse look like a piker. Both the speech and the subsequent Transportation Act reflected the liberal influence of Supreme Court Justice Louis D. Brandeis, to whom he had been introduced by the subcommittee counsel and who had become his most revered Washington friend.

They also reflected the independent line he was taking with T. J. Pendergast and the big-money interests of his home state. He was not rejecting Pendergast; he was just, as he remarked, voting the way the people of

Missouri would want him to vote (or, as the boss would have put it, "being contrary again"). In fact, his continuing loyalty to Pendergast was a major element in the dramatic events that brought his first senatorial term to a close.

He begins his understated account of the drama with a reference to his Missouri colleague, Senator Bennett Clark:

> Senator Clark, having come to the Senate in 1933, a few days before the Democratic Administration took over, had succeeded in filling all Federal patronage appointments before I arrived. Both District Atorneys were recommended by him as were U.S. Marshals and Collectors of Revenue for the Eastern and Western Districts of Missouri. None of these gentlemen were in sympathy either with me or the policies of the Roosevelt Administration— Sen. Clark having taken at the beginning of the Roosevelt term a stand with the opposition.
>
> So when the terms of the District Attorney and U.S. Marshal came to an end in 1937 I recommended other men for their places. But the vote fraud scandals and Pendergast's troubles were rife about that time and the Administration didn't have the nerve to back up its friends in Missouri. . . .

The Pendergast "troubles" had their origin back in 1929 when a group of insurance companies boosted Missouri fire insurance rates by more than 15 percent. The State Insurance Superintendent objected, and a federal court impounded the extra money pending a judgment on its disposition.

The case dragged on, and by 1935 the sequestered cash was nearing $10 million. Pendergast, who had suffered huge gambling losses, finally sent his State Insurance Superintendent to the companies with a proposal to end the legal impasse. The companies listened and not long afterward were awarded the lion's share of the impounded funds, with the rest being returned to the customers. Pendergast's secret payoff for arranging the settlement reportedly was made in several installments amounting in all to three quarters of a million dollars.

At this point, a driving, humorless millionaire nurseryman, a grower of Delicious apples named Lloyd Stark, came on stage.

> Along in February [Truman says], Lloyd Stark called me from his home . . . and informed me that he had a boy at Annapolis Naval Academy, that he was leaving home on a certain day to go and see the boy and that he would like very much to see me on the same trip. Of course I told him to stop in Washington on his way . . . and I'd be glad to see and talk to him as long as he liked. Mr. Stark had been one of my supporters in the bitter 1934 primary fight and I felt friendly and grateful to him.
>
> He came to see me sometime in February, 1935. His mission was to tell me that he wanted to be Governor of Missouri and that he knew he couldn't

make the grade unless he had the support of the Democratic organization in Kansas City and he wanted me to tell him how to get T. J. Pendergast to be for him.

I gave him the names of the leaders in sixty or seventy of the counties in Missouri who were my personal and political friends and suggested to him that he see them and have them write or call on Pendergast and tell him that they believed that Lloyd Stark would poll more votes in 1936 than anyone else in 1936 for Governor. . . .

In July . . . he told me that he'd seen Bennett Clark and that Bennett had agreed to go to New York to see Tom Pendergast in his behalf if I would go along. Tom had returned from one of his numerous trips to Europe on the big trans-Atlantic liners—the Roma or Queen Mary or the Normandie —and was at the Waldorf-Astoria.

I called Senator Clark and he confirmed the statement of Mr. Stark. Then I called Pendergast and told him that Clark and I would like to see him in New York the next day. He couldn't do anything else but see us. Two United States Senators can see anyone no matter who and T.J. was first of all a good politician. He was, as always with me, very cordial and said he'd be most happy to see Bennett and me.

We saw him next day in the Waldorf and Bennett told him that this man Stark had no political experience, that he was an egotist and not to be depended upon. I told Tom that I thought Stark was an honorable man and that he would make a good Governor. Which shows how easy it is to be fooled by your friends. Stark had neither honor nor loyalty. He should have been a member of the Spanish Inquisition or of the Court of Louis XI of France. Someday when I have time I'll write a character sketch of him that will be very interesting.

When the interview was over Pendergast called me aside and told me to tell Stark on the way back to Washington that if he would bring some good old country Democrats to Kansas City along in October [1935] and discuss his ambitions that he [Pendergast] would publicly announce for him for Governor. On the way back to Washington I told Stark what Pendergast had said to me. I almost had to leave the drawing room to prevent his hugging and kissing me. He appeared to be the most grateful man alive and told me that he'd do anything any time to help me.

He was elected Governor in 1936. Took office on Jan. 8, 1937. Came to see me as U.S. Senator just once after that. When he'd come to Washington as Governor of Missouri he'd call on the President, the Sec. of War or Navy and go out of town. On one occasion when he was calling on the Vice-President he stuck his head into the door of my reception room and told my secretary that certain rumors were about that he [Stark] was a candidate for the Senate in 1940. He assured my secretary that there was no truth in these rumors. I told the secretary that I'd bet my last dollar that Mr. Stark would try for my place in 1940.

This prediction was borne out and, when it was, things looked black indeed for Harry Truman. The seemingly invulnerable Pendergast had been stricken with a coronary and also with intestinal cancer. While he was immobilized, his followers outdid themselves to make him a present of the 1936 primary. They put over his candidate, Lloyd Stark, by a vote which, according to later calculations, would have been possible only if Kansas City had had at least a hundred thousand more voters than the census allowed it. U.S. Attorney Maurice Milligan, still pursuing his criminal investigations, added this phenomenon to his list of things to be examined.

Once settled in as Governor, Stark wasted no time in divesting himself of past ties that might interfere with the brilliant future everyone was predicting for him. He appointed an anti-Pendergast election board; then he dismissed the boss's State Superintendent of Insurance and opened the way to the discovery of the secret insurance company deal. He also backed the reappointment of Maurice Milligan as U.S. Attorney for the western district of Missouri.

By custom, Truman should have been the one to propose the candidate for that post, but Stark now was calling the shots in Missouri. He had ingratiated himself with Roosevelt to the point of being invited on pleasure cruises aboard the presidential yacht, a favor never accorded the Junior Senator.

So Milligan received the administration's endorsement and in February 1938, his name came before the Senate for confirmation. Truman, as Senator for the district in question, could have blocked the proceeding by stating that Milligan was personally objectionable to him. Instead, he got up and said that he was waiving that right because of the administration's attitude. He wanted the Senate to know, however, that, while believing that those guilty of voting fraud in Kansas City should be singled out and prosecuted, he also believed that Mr. Milligan, with the connivance of a couple of rabid Republican judges, was conducting a witch-hunt.

He must have realized that it would look as though he were trying to cover up the corruption of his own political organization. But he plowed ahead anyway, while his colleagues heard him out mostly in silence. When the vote was called, his was the only nay.

After Stark's firing of the Superintendent of Insurance, federal sleuths stumbled on the trail that led to the insurance bribe, and in April 1939 Tom Pendergast was indicted for income tax evasion. His followers, most of whom, including Truman, had not guessed the excesses his gambling addiction had led to, were doubly shocked when he withdrew his original plea of not guilty and threw himself on the mercy of the court.

With his sentencing (fifteen months in prison, a $10,000 fine and payment of a half-million-dollar tax bill), together with the disclosure that the vaunted "money-saving" accounting system of City Manager Henry McElroy concealed millions of dollars' worth of pilfering, the whole Pendergast machine began to fall apart. Friends urged Truman to save himself by standing on his own record, but he refused, saying he was not the kind to desert a sinking ship.

Following Stark's announcement that he was running for Junior Senator, the Missouri press, led by the state's two biggest newspapers, gave him enthusiastic support. It was intimated that he also had Roosevelt's. Truman gathered as much himself when he received a presidential message offering him an appointment to the Interstate Commerce Commission, a broad hint that his chances of returning to the Senate were considered minimal. Although inclined to think so, too, he mustered up spirit enough to reply that he was going to be a candidate for reelection if the only vote he got was his own.

His 1948 campaign against Thomas E. Dewey usually is thought of as the toughest of his career, but in some respects this 1940 primary was even more difficult. After all, in 1948 he was President of the United States, in itself no mean asset. As Senator—Pendergast's Senator—he appeared to have no assets, only debits. When he got a group of his friends together to discuss campaign strategy, about half of them showed up—to tell him he didn't have a prayer of winning. He had no political organization behind him; at first he didn't even have the money to buy stamps for campaign mailings.

And he was further handicapped by his principles. In his opening campaign speech, for instance, he plunged into the troubled waters of civil rights. He was just following the lead of the Constitution of the United States, he explained, but some political wiseacres would have none of that. They said he was making a desperate bid for the black vote. The only trouble with their theory is that in the Missouri of those days any single black vote, so gained, would have been at the risk of losing a dozen white ones.

"And he wouldn't in his campaign say one thing about what he'd done as Senator," Colonel Burrus noted. "He'd say what the Democratic Party had done. I was with him. I said, 'Harry, when are you going to say something about yourself?' 'I'm not going to!' 'Well, when are you going to let us say something about you?' 'You can't say it while I'm on the platform. I'm talking about the party. If they can't understand what I'm talking about and that I had a part in it, then I never will get the nomination. . . .' "

Worse still, from the point of view of his entourage, was his refusal to take advantage of a letter he had received from Lloyd Stark in 1935, after the Waldorf meeting with Pendergast. It brimmed with gratitude over the boss's promise of support. "You can slaughter him with it," his friends told him, but Truman shook his head—no, it wouldn't be right.

How could a man like that expect to win against not only one but two opponents (by this time Maurice Milligan also had decided to run), doughty slayers both of the monster Pendergast, and both now promising to rid the state of the monster's last ally, Truman? Obviously he couldn't, and yet, as he says in his sketch:

> I was nominated by a plurality of 8400 votes in the August primary, after the most bitter, mud-slinging campaign in Missouri's history of dirty campaigns.
>
> At 11:00 o'clock on the night of the primary vote I went to bed 11,000 votes behind and supposedly defeated. The K.C. Star and the St. Louis Post-Dispatch had extras out telling how happy they were and safe Missouri was from my slimey [sic] person as Senator. A lying press cannot fool the people. I came back to the Senate and the double-crossing ingrate of a Governor was sent back to the nursery.
>
> The District Attorney, Mr. Milligan, had turned on all the power of his office to try to find something wrong with my record as a public official. Of course, he couldn't find it but he made the same bitter campaign as if he had found it. The violently partisan Republican Federal Judge at Kansas City finally had to tell him to stick to facts.

The victory seemed a miracle, and in a way it was, even though some of the reasons for it can be distinguished. One reason was Stark's overweening ambition. While running for Senator, he rubbed a lot of home folks the wrong way by also trying to win the Democratic nomination for Vice-President of the United States.

Then, with Milligan's entrance, the contest took on the split-vote configuration of the primary of 1934, and with the same result. And there was Truman's New Deal voting record (his Transportation Act was a factor), which earned him the support of organized labor. And finally there was the belated conversion to his cause of Bennett Clark.

Although never a close friend of his junior colleague, Senator Clark had gotten along with him well enough, certainly better than he could expect to do with the voracious Stark. When he finally was persuaded of this (and when his first choice, Milligan, obviously was getting nowhere) he let Stark feel the edge of his tongue, saying that Missouri's Governor appeared to be running for everything in sight, including the Archbishopric of Canterbury and the Akhund of Swat. More to the point, if less entertainingly, he helped to talk one of the St. Louis bosses, Robert E. Hannegan, into switching about half that city's Stark vote to Truman— just enough, as it turned out, to put the latter over the top.

The subsequent election, although less of a contest than the Democratic primary, was marked by just as much bitterness and dirtiness. Jackson County's anti-Pendergast presiding judge provided his share of both by expediting the foreclosure of a $35,000 mortgage, which had been taken out on the Truman farm two years before. Times were hard. Neither the Democratic senatorial nominee nor his brother had funds enough to save the property. Their mother and sister had to be moved from their home to a house in Grandview. All this was intended to lessen Truman's chances in the November election. But with the number of people who still were burdened with Depression-time debts, it aroused sympathy for him and contributed to his victory. Later, he charged that it led to the death of his eighty-eight-year-old mother, for in new, unfamiliar quarters she suffered a fall and broke her hip.

It is worth noting that Truman at this time (indeed throughout his political career) had no backup line of defense. When in trouble, most politicians are able to retreat to their professions, law or whatever, or their businesses or bank accounts. Until his retirement, Truman had nothing to retreat to but his grandfather's farm, which at this point he couldn't afford to save. So his ups and downs seem more suspenseful than most of his colleagues'. He was doing a high-wire act without a net: one slip and he was finished.

And now, while this dizzy year was drawing to a close, fate, as though to compensate for his domestic and political trials, dealt him a couple of extra ups. He was elevated to the highest Masonic post in Missouri, that of Grand Master of the Grand Lodge, and, on his return to the Senate, was given a standing ovation.

During his second senatorial term, Truman was admittedly more successful than he had ever been before. All his political skills, which had been developed and sharpened during eighteen years of public life, were called upon in organizing and chairing the Special Committee to Investigate the National Defense Program, the so-called Truman Committee, and the results transformed him into a nationally known figure.

Until it won acceptance, however, his committee was forced to run an obstacle course that made Christian's, in *Pilgrim's Progress*, seem downhill. To start with, it had the worst possible precedent in a similar committee which had investigated the Union's Civil War effort and which, General Robert E. Lee felt, was worth a couple of divisions to the South. Luckily, as a Civil War buff, Truman knew about the Civil War Committee on the Conduct of the War and was determined not to repeat its mistakes. But that was just the first of his problems.

Both the President and the administration leadership in Congress only permitted the Truman Committee to come into being as the lesser of two evils. By approving it, they managed to forestall the creation of a House committee which would have explored the same ground and, they feared, been unmanageable. To keep Truman's within bounds, they began by allowing it the tiniest of budgets.

Armed with $15,000, it set out to do battle with the Army and Navy, each of which wanted things its way, with conflicting government agencies, with industry, which was reveling in cost-plus defense contracts (the higher the costs, the higher the profits), and with labor, demanding its fair share of the plunder—in short, with the nation's whole pack of hounds in full bloodcurdling cry on the trail of the buck.

Truman and his little group of Senators not only steered their way safely through the pandemonium but managed in the process to form themselves into a machine more efficient than a lot of the war machines they were studying. In fact, before they were through, they set a record for congressional committees by issuing reports, not a single one of which expressed a minority opinion: they were all unanimous.

None of this, of course, has been neglected by the biographers and historians, but Truman's own view of it, as set forth in the penultimate pages of his autobiographical sketch, and the view of the committee's chief investigator, Mathew J. Connelly, lend the story some new touches:

> In 1940 was passed a Universal Service Law [Truman wrote]. I had been in the National Guard of Missouri from 1905 to 1917, in the first World War from 1917 to 1919, and an officer in the Field Artillery Reserve from 1919 to 1940. I had been training reserve officers at camps and in nightschools from 1920 to 1940. So I went down to see the Chief of Staff, Gen. Marshall, and told him I'd like to quit the Senate and go into service as a Field Artillery Colonel and an instructor in F.A. tactics. He asked how old I was and I told him I was 56 years old. He pulled his reading glasses down on his nose, grinned at me and said, "We don't need old stiffs like you. This will be a young man's war." He was right, of course, but it hurt my feelings, and I decided to do something for the war effort on a constructive basis.
>
> After we had appropriated about twenty-five billions of dollars for national defense, I took my old coupe and began inspecting camp construction and naval installations from Maine to Florida and from Pennsylvania to New Mexico, California, Washington and along both borders north and south.

Some 30,000 miles were covered.[1] This while the bitter Missouri election campaign was on also.

On February 18, 1941, I made a statement to the Senate on what I'd seen and asked that a special committee be authorized to look into defense expenditures. I believe that statement resulted in the savings of billions of the taxpayers' money and thousands of lives of our fighting men. A great deal of difficulty was experienced in getting the Committee on Audit and Control to authorize funds after the Military Affairs Committee had decided that a Special Committee to Investigate the National Defense Program ought to be authorized.

James F. Byrnes was Chairman of the Committee on Audit and Control. He was a very cagey politician and he was afraid that the Junior Senator from Missouri wanted a political weapon, although he'd just been returned to the Senate for another six years and could afford to be a statesman for at least four years. Mr. Byrnes finally agreed to give the Committee the munificent sum of $15,000 to investigate the expenditures of $25,000,000,000.

The Vice-President appointed the committee of seven senators [2] with Truman as chairman and we went to work. . . . We made no statement unless we had the facts. We wanted no one smeared or whitewashed and after two years of very hard work the Committee had a national reputation for energy and integrity. . . .

We saw the scamy side of the war effort. We had to investigate crooked constructors on camp construction, airplane engine manufacturers who made faulty ones, steel plate factories, which cheated, and hundreds of other such sordid and unpatriotic ventures. We investigated procurement, labor hoarding, Army and Navy waste in food and other supplies. But when we were coming to our conclusions, we all decided that by and large the greatest production and war preparation job in history had been done.

Due to the fact that the Chairman was in charge, presided most of the time at the meetings of the Committee, he naturally was most mentioned in connection with the hearings and findings of the Commitee. When the 1944 election was approaching, mention began to be made about Truman for Vice-President. Every effort was made by me to shut it off. I liked my job as a senator and I wanted to stay with it. . . .

In 1941 Senator Lister Hill of Alabama advised his friend Mathew J. Connelly to see Senator Truman, who was beginning to assemble the staff of the Special Committee to Investigate the National Defense Program. Connelly at the time was angling for a job as a White House troubleshooter and did not think that he would be interested in anything else. Nevertheless, he made an appointment to talk to Truman:

---

[1] A reprise of his 24,000-mile trip as presiding judge. This one, too, he paid for himself.
[2] The committee later was enlarged to ten senators, and after its first report its budget was raised to $100,000.

"I walked into his office; I had never met him. So he said, 'I know all about you. I know what you did in Missouri, Chicago, and other committees you've been on.[3] We have a very peculiar situation here. I have been authorized to become chairman of this committee. However, it has not been determined what our appropriations are going to be. I do not know what I can pay you, but I will say this to you: if you go along with me, you will never have any reason to regret it.'

"I replied, 'Senator, I came in here to say no, but the way you talk is refreshing in Washington and you've got yourself a deal.'

"I knew in the begining that Jim Byrnes didn't want Truman to have the committee, and Jim Byrnes was chairman of the committee which made appropriations for senate committees and he gave Truman $15,000 as the appropriation for the committee. Truman talked to me about it and said, 'What are we going to do to build up a staff on $15,000?'

"So I suggested to him that he call the department heads and place his personnel on the department payrolls, which we did. I went on the National Housing payroll. I don't know what payroll Clark [4] went on . . . but I know that we were first put on the department payrolls, until Truman got more money. Then we switched to the committee payroll. . . .

"Truman thought that some improvement could be made on what the Army was doing with Army construction, camp construction, and that was the first phase of the investigation. . . . But he did not want any part of telling the armed services how to run the war. He thought that should be left to the generals. . . .

"I personally conducted the initial investigations of new Army camp construction. . . . The first thing I would do was report to the camp commander. Then I would look at the records—what the accomplishments were, what the initial cost estimate was, what it developed into. They appointed architect-engineers to help the camp commander build the camp, and these were civilian engineers, so, of course, they were always in a hassle with the brass, and after I got the commander's position, then I would talk to the architect-engineers and they were never hesitant to tell me what the truth was, what was going on at that base. So after getting the Army's side and the civilian engineers' side, I got a pretty good picture of what was going on at that camp site. And on that I based my report."

One of Connelly's investigations sounds like the start of a private-eye novel:

[3] On these committees, Connelly had investigated the welfare program and campaign expenditures.
[4] Charles Patrick Clark, the committee's associate counsel, was the next man hired, after Connelly.

"Senator Truman called me one morning, and he said, 'I want you to go to Kentucky. I was talking to Senator Barkley. Apparently Happy Chandler [5] is involved in some difficulty.'

"So I said, 'What's it about?'

"He said, 'Oh, something about the opponent who's running against him for election—has accused him of having a swimming pool built of critical materials that a contractor supplied.' He said, 'I know that Barkley wants Chandler back in the Senate.'

"I said, 'Oh, one of those.'

"He said, 'Well, you go see Chandler and get his side of it.'

"Which I did. Chandler suggested I contact some people he knew down there and they could fill me in on what the story was. . . .'"

In Kentucky, Connelly first called on the lawyer who was running against Senator Chandler and had brought the charges. Turned out the man had never seen the swimming pool; but he had photographs of it and had heard that it contained materials banned from that kind of use by the Office of Price Administration.[6]

From Lexington, where this interview took place, Connelly moved on to Louisville:

"I met the contractor, went through his records, went out to see the pool, and while I was there with the state chairman of the Democratic Party, Chandler's wife came out—she didn't know me—and she said:

" 'Bob'—his name was Bob Humphreys, he was the state chairman— 'what are you going to do about these OPA [6] people? They're raising hell about me getting a couple of new tires.'

"Well, the state chairman practically went into the pool himself with this little demonstration. I ignored it, it was all right with me, so we left there and he said, 'Oh, brother!'

"I said, 'I know what you mean. I didn't hear it.'

"Well, after getting the whole thing wrapped up, I got all the records, found out that the steel in the pool was, you know, used steel—it wasn't good for structural steel, it had been used before. So I got the thing all wrapped up, came back to town and I reported to Truman directly. He said, 'Well, Barkley is edgy. What are we going to do?'

"I said, 'Well, all right. Now,' I said, 'when you report to the Senate that there has been an investigation, that you just got a personal report on the investigation, I would suggest that after you go on the floor, let me

---

[5] Albert B. Chandler resigned as Governor of Kentucky in 1939 and was appointed to fill a Senate vacancy. In 1940, he was elected to the remainder of his Senate term and in 1942 was reelected to a full six-year term.

[6] The Office of Price Administration set wartime prices and rationed scarce items, such as tires and steel.

write out a statement for Senator Hatch, the father of the Clean Politics Bill, and let him follow you and read his statement.'

"So I dictated this statement to one of the girls, and I went over and gave it to Senator Hatch. Truman made a little speech about the pool. Hatch followed with the statement I had written, then Barkley took over from there. Well, all it meant was I put holy water in the swimming pool, but that was what you call politics."

The Truman Committee, in Connelly's estimation, was unusual "because there was very rarely a congressional committee to make any kind of report which is unanimous, and I think it's a great tribute to the then Senator Truman that he was able to handle the members of the committee, up to ten senators, in such a way that prevented or didn't make possible a minority report. For in his ability to get along with other senators, give each one credit for his part in the activities without any discrimination regardless of politics, was real statesmanship. . . ."

He had good relations with the staff, too. "They all liked Senator Truman because he gave them respect. He was never an authoritative type chairman. He'd say, what is this? and let them explain to him what they thought, and if he didn't agree, he'd tell them, and tell them why. So the relationship between Truman and the staff, I would say, was excellent. Because of the work of that committee, and during the proceedings of the committee, in a press poll he was considered to be one of the top ten senators in Congress." [7]

[7] After three years as chief investigator for the Special Committee, Connelly became Truman's vice-presidential secretary and then his presidential appointments secretary. He was in charge of the Truman train in the famous whistle-stop campaign of 1948. In 1953 he went into the public relations business in New York and in 1955, along with T. Lamar Caudle, assistant attorney general under Truman, was convicted on charges of conspiring to prevent an income tax evasion suit from being brought against a St. Louis shoe manufacturer, Irving Sachs. Connelly, seconded by Truman, claimed that he was a victim of a smear campaign being conducted against key members of the Truman administration by President Eisenhower's Attorney General, Herbert Brownell. Even the columnist Drew Pearson, never accused of being a partisan of theirs, publicly endorsed that claim. Nevertheless, despite lengthy appeals, both defendants received two-year jail sentences and fines of $2000. Six months after entering prison, Connelly was paroled, and in 1962 was given a full and unconditional pardon by President John F. Kennedy. He died six years later.

VIII

Vice-President

ROBERT E. HANNEGAN, THE ST. LOUIS BOSS, NEVER HAD ANY CAUSE TO regret the help he gave Missouri's Junior Senator in the 1940 primary. With Truman interceding on his behalf with Roosevelt, Hannegan rang up some kind of record for rapid political advancement. First he was named collector of internal revenue at St. Louis, then Commissioner of Internal Revenue, then chairman of the Democratic National Committee. In the last assignment, he was able to show his gratitude and did so handsomely. He more than any other one person was responsible for Truman's getting the vice-presidential nomination.

Since Roosevelt was going to run again and the war eclipsed all other issues, the main question confronting the Democratic National Convention of 1944 was that of the vice-presidency. The leading contenders at first were the incumbent, Henry A. Wallace, Senator James F. Byrnes of North Carolina, and Senator Alben Barkley of Kentucky. Roosevelt, who was loath to have his waning powers taxed by secondary matters, paid only fitful, seemingly capricious attention to the choice of a running mate. As a consequence, each of the main candidates got the impression that he was favored.

To the political bosses, the vice-presidency seemed of critical importance because of their suspicion that the President might not last out a fourth term. The kind of man they wanted for the job was an approachable, dependable one, who might have a chance of holding together the agglomeration of diverse elements the party had become in the last dozen years. None of the front runners seemed to fit the bill: Barkley they thought too old; Wallace, too far left; and Byrnes, too far right. Thus at the center of things was a vacuum which Hannegan proceeded to fill with Truman. But it took some masterful politicking to do it. Wallace, for instance, kept showing a lot of strength, and on the other side, as between the elusive Roosevelt and the contrary Truman, it was a question which was the harder to deal with.

"I tried in every possible way at Chicago in 1944 to prevent my nomination for the Vice-Presidency," Truman later declared in a letter to a friend. "When Mrs. Truman, Margaret and I were on the point of leaving Independence for Chicago on Friday before the Convention of 1944, a phone call came from Washington. It was the Hon. James Byrnes. He asked me to nominate him for Vice-President. He informed me that President Roosevelt had endorsed him. I told him if Roosevelt had endorsed him I'd be glad to do what he asked.

"Before I could reach the car, the phone rang again and Sen. Barkley asked me to nominate him. I told him of my conversation with Jimmy Byrnes. . . ."

The ensuing events are recounted in the final pages of his autobiographical sketch:

> I spent a most miserable week in trying to stave off the nomination. I had breakfast with Sidney Hillman [1] and tried to get him to support Byrnes. Spent an hour with Phil Murray [1] and Whitney [1] of the Railroad Trainmen on the same mission. Had breakfast with William Green [1] to ask his support of Byrnes. They all refused to support him. Each one of them except Green said he was for Wallace, but that he would take me if he had to. Green said he was never for Wallace and wanted me all the time. I told all of them I was positively not a candidate, that I liked my senatorial position and felt that I was making some contribution to the war effort. . . .

Eddie McKim picks up the story:

"In June or July 1944, Mr. Truman suggested to me that I arrange to be at the Democratic National Convention in Chicago. As he said, he was having John Snyder and me there to block any attempt to make him the vice-presidential nominee."

McKim arrived in Chicago on the Monday the convention opened:

"There was quite a bit of political activity all during that day. And during the day, John Snyder and I went into one of the bedrooms and discussed the situation. It looked to us like Truman was the only one that could be nominated. We decided we'd better tell him about it, because we didn't want to be in the position of blocking something that would

---

[1] All labor leaders.

interfere with a man's destiny. So we told him how we felt and he said, no, he didn't want it."

McKim and Snyder then asked Roy Roberts, editor of the *Kansas City Star*, to add his voice to theirs:

"I think it was either Monday night or Tuesday night that Roy Roberts, John Snyder and I got Truman in a room around midnight. We explained the situation to him, and he said, 'I'm still not going to do it.'

"Finally I said, 'I think, Senator, that you're going to do it.' He got a little belligerent with me and said, 'What makes you think I'm going to do it?' I said, 'Because there's a little ninety-year-old mother down in Grandview, Missouri, who would like to see her son President of the United States.' And with that the tears came into his eyes and he stomped out of the room, he wouldn't speak to me."

Meanwhile, Hannegan had been trying to get Roosevelt to back Truman. Before the convention, Matt Connelly says, "Hannegan, Ed Pauley, who was then treasurer of the National Committee, Frank Walker, who had been Postmaster General and also chairman of the National Committee, had a meeting with Roosevelt at the White House, and Roosevelt was very reluctant, but they finally agreed that he would take Truman, but Truman was not his first choice."

His first choice was Henry Wallace, and later he added U.S. Supreme Court Justice William O. Douglas, with Truman in third place.

"During the convention," Connelly continues, "Roosevelt went through Chicago but didn't go to the convention. The train was parked in the railroad yards in Chicago and he was transferred to [a train for] the West Coast. . . . So Hannegan went down and asked him to give him a letter that Hannegan could take to the convention and Roosevelt agreed. Roosevelt dictated a letter to his secretary, Grace Tully, listing the three candidates for Vice-President who would be acceptable to him."

Douglas was number one on the new list, Wallace two, and Truman still three.

"Hannegan," Connelly says, "got to Grace Tully and rearranged the names and put Truman on top. Then Hannegan went to the convention with that letter. Now, the Wallace crowd was well organized and they stampeded that convention and almost got Wallace, but Hannegan finally cut the thing off before they could have a vote, and partly through Jackson from Indiana, the chairman.

"Sam Jackson didn't want to quit. Hannegan said, 'You recess the convention or I'll throw you off that platform.' He [Jackson] had the organist playing 'Iowa.' [2] Neale Roach, who is in public relations now in Washing-

[2] The rousing song of Wallace's home state.

ton, went up to the organ and on Hannegan's instructions pulled a fire ax off the wall and cut the cable. That's how close it was. So that's the story of how Truman became Vice-President. . . ."

But not quite the whole story.

> On Thursday night [Truman's sketch goes on], after the Convention had adjourned because of a gallery-paid demonstration for Wallace, some of the Southern Democrats, Hannegan, Walker and Ed Pauley told me that I was going to be responsible for a split in the Democratic Party, which would result in the election of the New York Governor.[3]
>
> Maryland's Governor, the Governor of Oklahoma, Harry Byrd, the Junior Senator from Mississippi, and Gov. Graves of Alabama, along with Tobin and William Green told me that they could all take me and save the Party. . . .

Even that was not enough. The final persuader was a telephone call from Hannegan to Roosevelt, who by then was in San Diego. As Hannegan held the receiver away from his ear, the President could be heard saying that if Truman wanted to break up the party with a war on, that was his responsibility. Truman then, in his words, "caved in." He reluctantly asked Byrnes to release him from his promise and Byrnes with even more reluctance agreed. (Later Truman came to believe that the North Carolina Senator's purpose in choosing him as his nominator had been to eliminate a possible rival.)

The last two paragraphs of Truman's sketch read:

> On the second ballot, I was nominated. Had no acceptance speech ready and accepted in sixty words. Held a press conference after the convention adjourned . . . and slipped out of town in my own car Saturday at noon and went home to Independence. They put on a big show and reception there and shortly after that we came back to Washington.
>
> I resigned as Chairman of the Special Committee over the protest of every member on it. They passed a resolution which makes me blush every time I read it, and my career as a candidate for Vice-President of the United States began. It was successful, and the President and I were sworn in at the White House on January 20, 1945. . . .

Hannegan later summed it all up by saying that he hoped his epitaph would credit him with having kept Henry Wallace from becoming President of the United States.

After the inaugural on January 20, 1945, Truman telephoned his mother

---

[3] The Republican candidate, Thomas E. Dewey.

in Grandview and asked if she had listened to the ceremony on the radio. She said she had and added, "Now you behave yourself up there, Harry." To which he replied, "I will, Mamma."

However, a week later he flew out to Kansas City to attend the funeral of Thomas J. Pendergast and in doing so gave a lot of people an excuse to say that he already was misbehaving.

In Independence I came across two appropriately strange accounts of events in Truman's dreamlike interlude as Vice-President. The first is made up of recollections of Harry Easley, a Missouri businessman, politician and friend of Truman:

"He called me up here at the bank right after the election. It must have been just a few days, because it seems to me that the old Battery D crowd had this reunion—they used to always have it on Armistice Day. He called me from Washington and wanted me to come into Kansas City, be up there. He wanted to visit with me. I went up there, and they had the penthouse at the Muehlebach. And I stayed with him that night, I slept there with him. He told me, just lying there in bed after things quieted down, that he had been lonesome ever since the day they put the Secret Service on him, and that he had not yet seen the President at all.

"He told me that the last time he saw him that he had the pallor of death on his face and he knew that if he [Truman] lived that he would be President before the term was out. He said he was going to have to depend on his friends. He was talking about people like me, he said. We sat there and had quite a long deal. He never at any time told me that he didn't want the nomination, but he knew that he was going to be President of the United States, and I think it just scared the very devil out of him. . . .

"Later I went on back and went to the inaugural. The war was going on and they had the inaugural on the portico in the back there, and then they had a party afterwards in the White House. . . . We went to the White House, and they had a wheelchair for Roosevelt ready and had him in there; and they had these braces to put on him, and they also had that Inverness cape that he always wore. I remembered my conversation with Truman, and by God the President had the pallor of death on his face right then.

"For a long time they got away with the myth that there wasn't too much wrong with Mr. Roosevelt. They'd never let anybody see his lower extremities, you know, he was always swinging on his arms. But—what the hell was his doctor's name? McIntire—they got around and they were going to put these braces on his legs, and he said, 'Just get the hell out of the way.

I've stood on my own feet three times before and I'm not going to stand on those things this time. You just take me out there and I'll do my talking.' And they did.

"They just rolled him out in the chair, you know, and he never did put those braces on. I imagine they were painful, a man as big as he was. But I've always thought about that, because that inaugural was no sooner over than he went to Teheran.[4]

"Then, when he came back, I happened to be in Washington. When he came back, he had that stroke on the *Augusta* and it circled at sea—the war was going on—and it circled out there for quite a long time until they found out, and then they waited for the air force to come out there and escort them on in. Mr. Truman, I've just conjectured, he couldn't have seen the President over three or four times, because I happened to be there at that time and he told me that they got the word that Roosevelt had had this stroke. [Not the one that killed him.] This was on the way back from Teheran.

"Truman told me that Sissy Roosevelt,[5] she was the only one really close to the President. He told me that there wasn't a lot of affection in the family. I guess the President was kind of estranged as far as Mrs. Roosevelt was concerned. It was just one of those things. But this Sissy could do more with him than anyone. And they flew her down to meet the boat when it got in. Mr. Truman said that she brought that old man out of it and that he didn't look too bad at all—they kept him sort of sequestered. But he never brought Truman up to date on anything, nothing, apparently. Then he went on down to Warm Springs and died in April, the 12th of April.

"Well, the inaugural was in January, I've forgotten what date. So, you see, I've always thought about Truman's anguish, when he made that statement about the load of hay falling on him.[6] I can sure as hell understand it, because he didn't have any guidance into that job or anything else. It was just fortunate that he had the senatorial background and the experience that he did before he fell in there. I never did hear him say that he didn't want the nomination, and I think he thoroughly enjoyed it after he got in there. . . ."

Adding a footnote to Easley's remarks, Ethel Noland said:

"It was a long time before there was any question of the President's [Roosevelt's] health failing. A short time before his death Bess wrote to me,

[4] He means Yalta, where Roosevelt met Churchill and Stalin in February 1945.
[5] FDR's daughter, Anna.
[6] Truman to the press: "Boys, if you ever pray, pray for me now. I don't know if you fellows ever had a load of hay fall on you, but when they told me yesterday what had happened, it felt like the moon, the stars and all the planets had fallen on me."

'People say the President is in failing health, but I don't believe it.' She sat next to him at dinner the week before. 'There's nothing the matter with him, except that I think he's getting a little deaf. A lot of us are getting a little deaf, so I don't think that's anything.'

"But it wasn't very long until you could see he was failing. You could see it in his pictures. I think the truth of it was that Bess didn't want to think that he was in failing health. There was a little wishful thinking there, I think, because it was the least of her desires to be the first lady."

The second odd account of history in the making is Eddie McKim's, and it concerns the day Roosevelt died. McKim was in Washington on a business trip that April 12, 1945, and met Truman in the office of the Secretary of the Senate, Leslie Biffle:

"Going back from Les Biffle's office to what Truman then called his 'gold-plated office,' which was the Vice-President's office right behind the Senate Chamber, he said, 'Don't you think we ought to have a little game tonight?'

"I said, 'Yes, I think so. Where do you want to play?'

"He said, 'Down in your room.'

"I said, 'The room I've got I have to have a shoe horn to get in it myself; it was the only thing I could get, but I'll go see Bill Davis, the manager of the hotel, and see if I can get bigger quarters.'

" 'Well,' he said, 'you do that.'

"And he gave me a list to call to get them for the game.

"And he said, 'How's your whiskey supply?'

" 'Well,' I said, 'it's nonexistent.'

" 'Well,' he said, 'I've got some new whiskey over in the Senate Office Building office,' and he said, 'You go over there and get what you think we'll need. There's a case of scotch that Jimmy Cromwell sent me'—he was then the ambassador to Canada—'and there's a case of bourbon there,' and I think he said it was Barney Baruch who sent it to him.

"Anyway, after I left Vice-President Truman there, I went over to the Senate Office Building and got the liquor and took a cab down to the Statler Hotel. I went to the manager, Bill Davis, and told him my story, and that I'd have to have more room. So he gave me a suite. He sent a bellboy up to transfer my stuff from the room I was in. He sent up a green poker table, and I got all the mix and the ice and everything up there—got all set for it. Then a friend of mine, Fletcher Neal from Omaha, quite an ardent Democrat, came by to see me and he said, 'The V-P says to tell you that the Senate has adjourned. He is going over to Sam Rayburn's office, then he's coming over here to the Senate Office Building and sign the mail. He's got a call from the White House he'll have to answer that, and after that we'll be down, but we'll be a little bit late.'

"So that was O.K. I was sitting there talking to Mr. Neal when the phone rang again, and it was Bill Davis, the hotel manager. And he said, 'I don't want to start any rumors and I don't want to spread any. I just thought I'd tell you that one of our maids was cleaning up the room of a Government man, he had a shortwave radio and it could be that you won't have any party tonight.'

"Well, then the thought struck me, 'He had a call from the White House.'

"And Davis said, 'If there's anything to it, it will be on the radio.'

"And when I put down the phone I walked over and turned on the radio and they're swearing in Mr. Truman at the White House, because the White House had caught him in Sam Rayburn's office and hustled him right down there. So I want to tell you, I got the jitters right then and right quick. I tried to get Neal to take a drink with me, but he wouldn't, but I took a good stiff one. In a little while, Neal left and Harry Vaughan and Matt Connelly came in. We're sitting around there wondering what to do. We had to make some calls and call off all the poker party and finally my phone rang another time, and I was getting a little fed up with answering the phone, having the jitters anyway, and this voice said, 'Eddie?'

"And I said, 'Mr. President.'

"He said, 'I guess the party's off. They've got me fenced in out here. Have you seen Matt or Harry?'

"And I said, 'They're both sitting right here.'

"He said, 'Well,' he said, 'I want one of you to go over and take charge of the Senate Office Building office tomorrow, and I want the other two of you at the White House.'

"I said, 'We've discussed that and Harry Vaughan will go over to the Senate Office Building.'

"And he said, 'You and Matt show up at the White House at nine o'clock.'

"And I said, 'How do we get in?'

"And he said, 'You'll get in.'

"So Matt came down to the hotel the next morning and we walked over there together. Incidentally, we had no trouble getting in.

"So we were shown into the presidential office and the President got up from this big desk and walked over to me and he said, 'Eddie, I'm sorry as hell about last night.'

"And I said, 'Why?'

"He said, 'Well,' he said, 'you've been in on everything else and you missed the big event, and I thought somebody had called you but nobody had.'

"And I said, 'Mr. President, it doesn't count what's gone before, what counts is what happens now.'

"So he walked back to his desk and sat down and I stood right where I was.

"He said, 'Do you have to stand there?'

"And I said, 'Well, Mr. President, I suddenly find myself in the presence of the President of the United States and I don't know how to act.'

"And he said, 'Come on over and sit down.'

"I sat down and he said, 'Do you have to go home?'

"And I said, 'Well, you know that I was leaving this afternoon for Omaha.'

" 'Well,' he said, 'I need you. Stick around awhile; I need some help.'

"I said, 'O.K., sir, I'll stay as long as you want.'

"So that was that."

If Truman comes through in this account as remarkably self-possessed, it is McKim's own jitteriness that makes him seem so. In fact, Roosevelt's death left him more uncertain, even humbler, than he'd been on his first arrival in Washington a decade earlier. His remark to the press about the load of hay was no exaggeration. He was so overcome that two of his friends, Senators Barkley and Aiken, urged him to buck up before it became catching.

Of course, he did buck up, as he'd always done and in the same way, by working his head off. It was a long haul, though, because, except for the knowledge of governmental operations he had acquired in his Senate jobs, he was in the dark. All he knew about the atomic bomb, for instance, was that something of great importance to do with the war was in progress offstage somewhere. Foreign affairs also were a blank to him. And he had inherited a government machine that testified to Roosevelt's talent for innovation but to the uninitiated looked like a monstrous Rube Goldberg invention.

IX

Money

BEFORE GETTING INTO TRUMAN'S PRESIDENCY, IT MIGHT BE WORTHWHILE to spend a moment or two more on his financial vicissitudes, particularly on the fortunes of the Grandview farm after the $35,000 mortgage on it was foreclosed in August 1940. Charles F. Curry, a Kansas City real estate man and longtime friend of Harry and Vivian, took an interest in the delinquent property and gives the best available account of what happened to it:

"I became aware of it [the foreclosure] when the court decided to publicize the situation that Harry Truman had borrowed money from the County School Fund on his farm, and had not paid the interest thereon, and had allowed it to go into default so that it had to be foreclosed upon, and that the farm had not been worth the money which was borrowed on it.

"In order to establish this situation, they conceived the idea of offering the farm at public sale in anticipation that it would not bring the amount at which the farm stood on the books of the School Fund. Such a sale would tend to establish the market value of the farm and the amount of money which the School Fund had lost and from which Mr. Truman had benefited by reason of the loan.

"By this time, Mr. Truman had become Vice-President of the United States and his opponents were trying in every way possible to embarrass him. Shortly before the date for which the sale was set, I was with a group of members of the Military Order of the World War discussing the situation. One of the group . . . commented that . . . they [the court] were not advertising the sale very widely and that it [the farm] would probably not bring the amount of the indebtedness thereon unless a group could be gotten together to bid it in at the cost price to the County. This, we all agreed, would be a fine thing for friends of Mr. Truman to undertake. The total amount due on the note together with accumulated interest amounted to about $43,000. . . .

"The County owned it [the farm] at this time. . . . Sealed bids were to be received and opened at a specified time by the court in special session. . . . It wasn't a sheriff's sale; it was a public sale by the county court of the entire farm, consisting of a 200-acre tract . . . and an 87-acre tract. . . . The Truman home place was located on the 87-acre tract. . . .

"I talked to Vivian about this sale and . . . Vivian explained that his mother wanted to live in the home place with the 87 acres, and that they were very anxious to keep it for her and could raise $20,000 to pay for it, but the court would not sell it separately. He said they would pay $20,000 for the home place if they could get somebody to buy the entire property and sell the home place back to them. . . .

"I agreed to undertake to get a small group together to underwrite the purchase. . . . Most of those with whom I discussed this thought it was a good plan . . . but did not have the cash. By the time of the sale, I had only two others committed . . . and I decided to go ahead and bid it in and take a four-sixths interest for myself.

"I advised Vivian that I would go ahead with the plan to purchase the farm at the sale, and that if I were successful I would sell him the 87 acres for $20,000. . . . I remember when we were drawing up the papers, this lawyer, whom I knew pretty well, said something about the farm, and I remarked that I'd never seen the place. He was astounded that I had not inspected the property, but I told him that I wasn't buying real estate for an investment; I was buying it to prevent misleading charges against the Vice-President of the United States. . . .

"I attended the sale and bid $43,000, which covered the full amount of the accumulated obligations on the original loan, including costs and interest. There were several other bids considerably lower in amount. The terms of my bid were a $10,000 deposit made with the bid; $20,000 in cash on delivery of deed, and a note for $13,000, secured by first deed of trust on the 200-acre tract. The 87 acres were to be deeded free and clear to allow for transfer of it free of any indebtedness upon payment of the $20,000 cash by the Trumans. The court accepted the bid and the purchase was consummated under its terms. Title was taken in the name of my bookkeeper. . . .

"It was not very long after the sale before Truman became President of the United States, and the Truman farm took on added historical value. It [1] was something that Mr. Truman might want to reacquire later, so we decided to hold it until such time as Mr. Truman might be able to work out a way to reacquire it. . . .

"I told Vivian to tell Harry that he could have the farm at our cost at any time that he wanted it. The word came back that he didn't want to ask us to hold it—that he wasn't in a position to purchase it at that time [2] but we continued to hold it off the market, believing that Mr. Truman would eventually want it.

"I never mentioned the matter of the sale of the farm to Mr. Truman personally. I was in Washington occasionally and I'd drop in to see him, but nothing was ever said about the farm."

Finally, in the spring of 1946, word reached Charles Curry (who appears to have conducted himself throughout with uncommon sympathy, skill and tact) by way of Vivian that President Truman would be interested in purchasing the 200-acre tract, and the sale was made for $10,000 subject to the lien of the $13,000 mortgage. The transaction was handled by lawyers and to the end went unmentioned between the two principal parties. But, Curry says, the President showed his appreciation in various ways, such as inviting him to White House functions.

There was another strange twist to the farm story. At the time of the 1940 senatorial election, one of the journalists who conspicuously attacked Truman over his borrowing from the School Fund was his former classmate, Charles Ross, then a writer for the *St. Louis Post-Dispatch*.

"Charlie Ross," Mildred Dryden said, "wrote an unkind article about the farm out there. I remember that distinctly. Mr. Truman was quite troubled about it. His family finally moved to town, his mother and his sister, Mary Jane. After moving into town, his mother fell. Mr. Truman was very bitter about the accident. It would not have happened if she had not been living in unfamiliar surroundings. I think Mr. Ross's article touched off the whole chain of incidents.

"Mr. Truman was more upset about his mother's accident than anything I ever saw during the time I was with him. He was very bitter toward Mr. Ross. And I was just amazed when he— Of course, those things, I guess, they finally work themselves out. After he became President, the

---

[1] The 200 acres still held by the Curry consortium.

[2] He was unable to purchase it even though he was President of the richest country in the world and the amount in question was $10,000, with modest mortgage payments.

first thing I knew Charlie Ross was over there as his Secretary of the Press. But I suppose those things were all forgotten. After all, that was Charlie Ross's job for a Republican paper. They had gone to school together and they had been old friends. Just one of those things. . . ."

Truman's financial worries included more than the farm. After his re-election to the Senate in 1940, he found that he could not go on supporting himself on his $10,000-a-year salary. There seemed to be two possible solutions: to follow the example of some other Senators and try the lecture circuit or to put his wife on his office payroll; she had been doing odd jobs for him anyway. Influenced perhaps by Matt Connelly's method of solving the Truman Committee's budget problem, he chose the second way. Mrs. Truman was allocated a salary of $4500 a year.

"The correspondence would come in," Colonel Burrus said, "and she'd sort it out, tell Mildred Dryden and the other secretaries how to answer it, maybe dictate notes for them. She was a kind of personal secretary. She knew the folks Mr. Truman wanted to recognize personally and those that might be recognized by a form letter, and she would winnow those things out that she knew he would either want to do himself or she could help get done for him."

"I would say," Mildred Dryden observed tactfully, "that she gave him a lot of very good advice."

Questioned by reporters about her secretarial duties, Mrs. Truman replied that she went over all her husband's speeches in advance.

Still, he must have been glad to discontinue the arrangement after becoming Vice-President, for he had criticized others for practicing nepotism.

Money problems followed Truman into the White House. Assistant Press Secretary Eben Ayers took note of some of them in his diary. His entry of June 23, 1952, for instance, is given over entirely to presidential finances:

"Howell Crim, the Chief Usher in the White House, told me an interesting story today. He said that he understood that when President Truman went to New York to review the St. Patrick Day parade in 1948 he sat with Governor Dewey in the reviewing stand and during the time they were together the President got into conversation with Dewey about the possibility of Dewey coming into the White House as President. Dewey at that time was a candidate for the Republican Presidential nomination, which he subsequently won, although he failed of election despite the confidence he and his followers had in his victory. He said that the President told Dewey of what he would be up against financially if he were to become

President and cited his own case, telling Dewey that he only had about $4500 left out of his salary at the time and that, while he had a grown daughter, Dewey had children and would be up against all the expenses that go with the office of President.

"Crim said that he understood that afterward Dewey got in touch with some of the other Republican leaders and they initiated the move to have the President's salary raised. The matter was brought to the attention of the Budget Bureau and James Webb, then Director of the Budget; and the President told Crim to cooperate with Webb. He said that he was called over to the Budget Bureau by Webb and the matter of increasing the President's salary was discussed. Crim said he pointed out that if any legislative action were taken it would have to be before the President-elect in November, 1948, took office, as a President could not accept an increase in salary during his term in office, but apparently Webb did not realize this and ordered his lawyers to check it up, which they did. As a result, legislation was introduced and passed in time for President Truman to get the increased salary [3] after he was inaugurated in January, 1949. Dewey, of course, did not benefit from the proposal, which he really initiated.

"Crim also told me some other interesting details of the manner in which White House bills are paid. He said that in the days previous to Truman, the expense of feeding the White House help, who had meals from the White House kitchens, was met by the President. He said he told President Truman that this amounted to around $30.00 a day and the President threw up his hands when told this. He said that he arranged so that this expense now is paid out of the Government funds except for two or three employees.

"He told of an occasion when the President asked him to buy some tooth paste and said for him to get it at the drug store up near where he formerly lived on Connecticut Avenue. Crim said of course he could buy tooth paste without going there after it. He spoke of another case when the President wanted him to get some shoe polish and told him to tell Mrs. Truman that he had ordered it. He said the President insists on paying for the pressing and cleaning of his clothes although there are valets in the White House.

"He said that when bills for White House supplies come in he goes over them and prepares the checks to the various concerns in a check book furnished by Mrs. Truman. The book shows no balances of funds. To each check he attaches the voucher or the bill and sends them back to Mrs. Truman. She or the President then sign the checks and they come back

[3] Truman in his second term received $100,000 p.a. in salary and $50,000 in expenses. Previously his salary had been $75,000 p.a.

to Crim, who mails them to the various stores and the check book is sent over to the President's personal secretary, Miss Conway.[4] He said Mrs. Truman goes over every bill thoroughly; that if there were a dozen of an item at a specified price each, she would multiply it out to check with the amount charged."

"When Mr. Truman came home [after the presidency], he didn't have anybody to do a single thing for him, drive his car, anything," Colonel Burrus said. "He had Rose Conway, but he paid her himself. The government didn't furnish him one nickel. He had $117-a-month retirement pay as a Colonel, retired, in the Army. They gave him no credit for being Commander in Chief,[5] but they retired him and that's as far as they would extend."

But in the later fifties, Truman finally emerged from the financial woods he'd been trapped in most of his life. His *Memoirs* and other literary efforts earned him over half a million dollars, to which was added an undisclosed but sizable amount (shared with his brother) from the sale to a developer of a major part of the Grandview farm.[6]

And in 1958, Congress voted to give ex-Presidents lifetime annual pensions of $25,000, free mailing privileges, free office space and up to $65,000 a year for office help (with a $10,000 annual allowance for their widows).

In looking through the material found in Truman's Library desk after his death, I came on a few tokens of his more abundant latter days. He'd gotten in the habit of jotting down notes to himself about the amount of cash he happened to be carrying around or had at hand. For instance, on January 25, 1961, he wrote:

"Hippocket [sic] $1000. Littlefold [sic], $9.00. Billfold $1996, silver $9.00. Total $3014."

At this time, in the early sixties, his bank balance, according to several self-addressed notes, hovered around $126,000, besides which he had holdings in securities and real estate and, of course, the recently voted pension.

So, to all the other traditionally American aspects of his career, there was added a happy financial ending.

---

[4] Rose Conway replaced Mildred Dryden in 1945.

[5] Ironically, Truman *as* Commander in Chief had made it possible for generals and admirals to retire on full pay, with aides to help them.

[6] The developer has transformed the storied site into a shopping center, which, except for the sign, Truman Corners, is indistinguishable from thousands of other such facilities across the country.

X

President

THE TRUMAN LIBRARY IN INDEPENDENCE IS CRAMMED WITH DOCUMENTS relating to his presidency. With one exception, the few given here were chosen because they illuminate unusual facets of the subject or well-known facets in an unusual way. The exception is a rough draft of a never-delivered farewell address, which he jotted down just before turning over the reins of government to Eisenhower. The address carries on from the point at which his previously quoted autobiographical sketch leaves off; and it is being used in the hope that it will map his presidential years well enough to indicate where the other comments and documents fit in. The latter are grouped under two headings: Life at the Summit and History Backstage.

Five days from today, at 12:00 o'clock noon, Jan. 20, 1953, I shall transfer the burden of the Presidency and return to Independence, Missouri, a free and independent citizen of the greatest republic in the history of the world.

Thirty years ago, on Jan. 1, 1923, I took the oath of office, assuming the responsibility for a county office to which I had been elected. I have been in elective office continually, except for two years, since that date—30 years.

It is a long time—but for me a happy one. My daughter was born in the years I suffered my only personal political defeat. Two years later I was back in the harness and have served continuously since. . . . The last seven years and nine months has been a period without a dull moment.

About 5:00 o'clock on the afternoon of that fateful April 12, 1945, the Senate recessed and I walked over to the office of the Speaker of the House,

Mr. Rayburn. I was informed as soon as I arrived that Mr. Early, the Press Secretary of the President, wanted me to call the White House. As soon as I could talk to Mr. Early, he told me to come to the White House as quickly as possible, to come in by way of the Pennsylvania Ave. entrance and to come to Mrs. Roosevelt's study.

When I arrived, I was informed that the President had passed away. It was a real shock when Mrs. Roosevelt made the announcement to me. The Secretary of State came in immediately, and after offering to do anything I could for Mrs. Roosevelt,[1] I told Mr. Stettinius to call a Cabinet meeting.

I was sworn in as President at 7:09 P.M. by the Chief Justice of the United States, Mr. Stone.

Things began to happen at once. The meeting of the United Nations had been called for April 25. I was asked if that meeting would go forward. I announced that it would.

After attending the President's funeral, I went to the Congress with a message. On May 7, Germany surrendered. The announcement was made on May 8, my 61st birthday.

Mr. Churchill called me shortly after that and wanted a meeting with me and Prime Minister Stalin of Russia. Later on a meeting was agreed upon and Stalin, Churchill and I met at Potsdam to implement the agreements made at Teheran and Yalta.

At the time, the Potsdam meeting was considered a success. Russia agreed to enter the Japanese war, the use of the atomic bomb was decided. We came away from the meeting feeling that we were well on the road to world peace. . . .

The above paragraph needs some annotation. Potsdam, for instance, was not considered a success for long. Truman says as much in the next paragraph. After mentioning Japan's surrender, he remarks: "Russia began to break agreements made with Great Britain and the United States one by one."

Similarly, the use of the Bomb was not decided on by the conferees at Potsdam but only by the Americans, among themselves. On July 16, the day after his arrival in Germany, Truman received word of the first successful nuclear explosion at Alamogordo, New Mexico. Churchill was informed of it, for the British had been involved in the project from the start. But what about the Russians? Had the time come to share the secret with them—and the world supremacy it seemed to mean?

Truman temporized. After waiting a week, he strolled over to Stalin and remarked that the United States had developed a new, highly destructive weapon. The Soviet leader was equally casual, saying merely that he hoped the thing would be used with success against the Japanese. Later

---

[1] Mrs. Roosevelt asked, "Is there anything *we* can do for *you*?"

events supported the guess that his spies already had broken the news to him.

The conference held other ticklish moments for Truman, as Harry Vaughan [2] makes clear:

"Mr. Roosevelt, even though he must have known that his health was not good, probably took the same attitude Mr. Truman did, just didn't want to think about it—if you don't think about it, it won't happen. He had never talked to Mr. Truman a minute on what happened at Teheran and what happened at Yalta and what happened at Casablanca, so Truman was not prepared at all. He didn't know any of the commitments we had made to Russia or to France or to Great Britain, and so when all of a sudden he had this job, he just had to do a terrific lot of reading and research. . . .

"This was April with the conference sixty days later, and that's an awfully short time to get prepared. It's unfortunate because—I can recall meetings at the Potsdam conference where some item would come up and Mr. Churchill said, 'Now Mr. Roosevelt promised me he would do so-and-so. . . . ' Well, you don't want to doubt Mr. Churchill's word, but Mr. Churchill is a man who is dedicated to do everything possible for the interests of the British Empire. I'm sure he demonstrated that sufficiently. Mr. Joe Stalin would say, 'Now the President Roosevelt promised that he would—' Everybody within the sound of his voice suspected that it was a lie from start to finish but how could you prove it? It was most difficult. . . ."

Even so, Truman was rather taken with Stalin, who reminded him of Tom Pendergast.

"I liked old Joe," he told the editors of his *Memoirs.* "I was very much impressed by him at Potsdam. When an agreement had been reached, the subject was never opened again. There was one instance that took place when the Roumanians and the Poles complained about their treatment by the Russians. They hadn't been able to hold free elections, and Churchill was taking up the cudgel for Roumania and Poland, as we all were at the time. Churchill said the treatment of the Poles particularly would not be pleasing to the Pope, and Stalin leaned over on his elbow and asked the Prime Minister how many divisions the Pope had.

"I think he, Stalin, was anxious at that time for world peace. I think he was of the opinion that recovery was what Russia needed more than anything else. But after he got back to Moscow and met with his people, he made up his mind that the agreements at Yalta and Potsdam were not what they wanted and broke them.

2 Vaughan went to Potsdam as Truman's military aide.

"I never saw him again after that, but I had several exchanges of messages with him, and he would nearly always do what I wanted him to do. I asked him to have Molotov sign the United Nations charter. I sent Harry Hopkins to Moscow to ask him for me. Molotov was balking, and Stalin instructed him to get the charter into being. And on one or two other occasions when there were hitches in the international setup I did the same thing. By special message to Stalin I succeeded in getting the United Nations program implemented, and then the Russians proceeded, shortly afterwards, to break every agreement made at Yalta and Potsdam, so there was nothing more I could do. But that is the reason for my being friendly with Stalin. I was always of the opinion that if our difficulties were faced openly and I had the opportunity to talk to him across the table that he would keep his agreements as long as I was President. After that, I don't know what he would have done."

We had trouble in Iran [the farewell address continues], in China, in Greece, in Italy, in France with the communists. Russia was at the root of all these troubles. In early 1946 we decided to help Greece and Turkey. Then came the Marshall Plan. . . . Then the Russians closed the road to Berlin. We and our allies supplied Berlin by air. China folded up as a result of the weakness of the Nationalist Government.

All these disturbances and many more were sparks that could start a world war. One of the worst of these was the division of India into two Commonwealth countries. Another was the war between Israel and the Arabs. The two bad situations were stopped without a world conflict.

The last and worst of the lot was Korea. But if we had not persuaded the United Nations to back up the free Republic of Korea, western Europe would have gone into the hands of the communists.

We inaugurated the Atlantic Pact, the Latin American Agreement and the Pacific Defense Agreement, all for the defense of the free world and to strengthen our friends and allies so as to prevent their invasion by Russia.

All these events required momentous decisions by the President of the United States. He made them and with but one idea in mind, eventual world peace.

In the inaugural address after my reelection in 1949 there was a fourth point, which suggested a plan for technical assistance to free nations to help them to help themselves and to have them develop their natural resources.

Point Four [3] is not an aid program in the sense that the Marshall Plan and the Mutual Defense programs are. It is a plan to furnish "know-how" from our experience in the fabulous development of our own resources. . . . Point Four will be our greatest contribution to world peace. . . .

All these emergencies and all the developments to meet them have re-

[3] The prototype of President Kennedy's Peace Corps.

quired the President to put in long hours, usually seventeen hours a day with no payment for overtime. But it was worth the effort, because results are showing.

We have 62½ million people at work—businessmen, farmers, laborers, white collar people—and all have better incomes and more of the good things of life than ever before in the history of the world. There hasn't been a bank failure in seven years. No depositor has lost a cent in that period.

The income distribution has been equitable and fair to all the population.

Many things have happened. The White House very nearly collapsed, the country has been through four campaigns, two congressional and two presidential. I have been to Mexico, Canada, Brazil, Puerto Rico and the Virgin Islands, Wake Island and Hawaii. I have visited every state in the Union but Vermont. Traveled 135,000 miles by air, 17,000 by ship and 77,000 by rail, but the mail always followed me and, wherever I happened to be, there the office of the President was.

I sign my name on the average 60 times a day, see and talk to hundreds of people every month, shake hands with thousands every year and still carry on the business of the largest going concern in the world.

I wish my successor every happiness and success. For the first time in the history of the executive branch an orderly turnover is being made. I have briefed my successor completely on all the affairs of the country both foreign and domestic. All Cabinet officers have been briefed as well as new heads of bureaus where they have been appointed. It has never been done before when the newly elected President has been of the opposite political party.

Mrs. Truman and I are leaving the White House with no regret. We've done our best in the public service we've rendered.

The sturdy rebuilt White House will stand for centuries, and so will the country itself. We feel we've made a contribution to the stability of the U.S.A. and the peace of the world.

LIFE AT THE SUMMIT

According to Harry Vaughan,[4] Roosevelt's failure to communicate with his new Vice-President was not exceptional: he did little confiding, seldom would delegate authority. "He was in effect his own secretary of each department and really his secretaries were only under-secretaries."

Truman's methods were more democratic. Although wishing to be kept

[4] In 1942, Vaughan gave up his job as secretary to Senator Truman in favor of active military duty. After serving a hitch in Australia, he returned in 1945 to become military aide to the Vice-President. Previously no Vice-President had had a military aide, let alone one who was a reserve, rather than regular, army officer. The appointment probably was justified, though, by the war and by Truman's special interest in military affairs; in any case, it was approved by General Marshall. When Truman succeeded Roosevelt, Vaughan continued to be his military aide, rising quickly to the rank of major general, reserve.

informed and reserving to himself the right to make decisions affecting policy, he let the members of his staff and cabinet pretty much run their own affairs.

When he had a matter to decide, he would ask for opinions of the staff, Vaughan said, and "He wanted everybody's expressed opinion. If somebody failed to say, he'd say, 'What do you think about this?' And then, after we'd get through, he'd say, 'I appreciate all your suggestions, but I'm going to do so-and-so.' And that was it. When everything is as free and above-board as that, you don't hesitate to express your honest opinion."

Truman's democratic ways also were appreciated by the White House employees. The Trumans, indeed, may have been—probably were—the family with the highest popularity rating among the help ever to live at 1600 Pennsylvania Avenue.

"The President," Vaughan said, "was on friendly terms with everybody. He spoke to everybody as he walked through—the gardener, the painters, he had something to say about what was going on. He treated everybody with a great deal of courtesy, which was a surprise to them, because Mr. Roosevelt, by and large, was too busy and preoccupied even to notice. Mr. Eisenhower treated everybody in the White House the same way he would treat a private soldier on sentry post; he would just pass him as if he was part of the furniture."

Vaughan went on: "There was another angle that I think was very fortunate. Mr. Truman never looked back over his shoulder. I can remember occasions—not many because I right soon learned not to do this—that I'd say, 'You know, that so-and-so we did yesterday or last week, I don't know. From the developments—seems like a mistake.'

"He'd say, 'We've got plenty of things to worry about and we'll have more to worry about tomorrow. I can't be concerned about what we did. If it's wrong, it was unfortunate, it was considered judgment, but we've got to do something else. There's nothing we can do about that.'

"And another thing that he would do that—for example, I'll just take as comparison Herbert Hoover. Now I think Herbert Hoover was a man who felt his obligations and his responsibilities very keenly, was very sincere and very conscientious, but he couldn't relax. I think another four years in the White House would have killed Mr. Hoover, because he was having his troubles and they got him down.

"Now Harry Truman, when he decides to lie down and take a nap, he can go to sleep in ninety seconds.[5] That is a fortunate thing, because when

[5] Truman had an abnormally slow heartbeat, which may have contributed to his equanimity.

you relax and you're refreshed and rested, why, you can tackle your problems a whole lot better. He was a hard worker, and he could cast off the cares and sit down for two or three hours and play poker and he wasn't thinking about a single thing except beating me out when I had a better hand than he did. . . ."

In his debut in these pages, Vaughan talked about the day in 1917 when he first met Truman. With a couple of other Army lieutenants, he arrived late at a brigade officers' call and fell afoul of the general who was conducting the meeting.

It would be hard to contrive a more appropriate entrance on stage for the sort of character Vaughan played in Truman's drama. And he went on playing it. Later, his talent for getting into trouble made him one of the focal points of the scandals that began to plague the Truman administration. Although these were minor as compared, say, with the Pendergast scandals (sometimes they served merely to camouflage political attacks), they nevertheless blew up a storm that might have broken a man less resilient than Truman. Lingering in the public mind, they did delay the recognition that subsequently came to him.

Anyhow, Vaughan was in the thick of them. He seemed to regard his job as principally one of doing favors for people. Bypassing all the stuffy rules and regulations, he could be counted on to get you a scarce seat on a plane, or a cabin on a ship, or theater tickets, or a tip on a horse, or gourmet food (along with a deep freezer to keep it in)—just name it and it was yours.

A Senate subcommittee, sniffing around the White House, got wind of these extracurricular activities of his and went baying after him but never quite managed to run him to ground. Apparently he performed his services for personal pleasure rather than gain, although he did not discourage contributions to the party coffers.

"He [Truman] always insisted that I shouldn't take it [the Senate investigation of Vaughan] to heart," he said, "because it was aimed at him really. That was the time that he developed that classical remark, 'If you can't stand the heat, get out of the kitchen.' I was getting a lot of abuse in the press about numerous matters and I went in one day to the President and said, 'It's more important that your administration have a little tranquility than it is that I stay around here, so if I should ask to go on inactive duty, it might relieve the situation.'

" 'Harry,' he said, 'you and I came in here together and we're going to leave together and I don't want to hear any more of this damned foolishness about you wanting to resign.'

"So I never brought the matter up again."

When he wasn't seeking it out or exposing himself to it, trouble sometimes seemed to go to considerable lengths to seek out Vaughan. There
was the time, for instance, when the President was returning from a
Southern trip and stopped on the way long enough to be awarded an
honorary doctorate by Baylor University in Waco, Texas.

His high school Latin and math teacher, Mrs. W. L. C. Palmer, had
helped to set the stage for this event, and her recollections of it contrast
rather strikingly with Vaughan's. Each time she would go to Waco to
visit her married daughter, she would sound the praises of her former
student, then in the White House. One of her listeners, Dr. Armstrong,
who was connected with the university, repeated some of her stories to
his colleagues, and they conceived the idea of presenting the honorary
degree. It seemed a natural thing to do since both Truman and Baylor
were Baptist.

"When they had it all arranged," Mrs. Palmer said, "I received an
invitation to the luncheon. . . . When we were seated, my little grand-
daughter, six years old, came in (I didn't know she was going to do this)
with a little box; she opened it and walked right up to the table where
Harry was and said, 'I have a flower for you.' It was a gardenia.

"Harry took it and put it in his lapel and said, 'Now put one right
there.' He wanted Martha Sue to kiss him on the cheek. So she has always
said that Harry Truman is her favorite person. . . .

"Oh," Mrs. Palmer added, "I forgot about that honorary degree. It was
wonderful to have the opportunity to see him receive it in the midst of all
those literary folks—a far cry from the time in 1901 when I saw him receive his diploma from Independence High School!"

Harry Vaughan's recollections of the event omit any mention of little
girls and gardenias. They begin: "As we got out of the cars to go into the
headquarters building at Baylor, somebody for some unaccountable reason
put a package in my hand and said, 'This is for the President.'

"Well, we went upstairs and in this headquarters building they had two
or three rooms upstairs, a sitting room and a bedroom that had been the
apartment of the original president of Baylor. It was furnished with furniture—they were very proud of the fact that this furniture had been brought
from New England by covered wagon out to Waco, Texas, and this was
the original furniture—colonial furniture. It was a great, big bed; one of
these beds that looked like it had about three feather mattresses on it.
It was about four and a half feet from the ground and very billowy-look-
ing with great big bolsters.

"We went in there to put down our hats and coats. I had this package
and I took the paper off it. It was a quart of Bourbon whiskey. I couldn't

conceive of what we'd do with it or where in the world we'd put it—it was like two tails on the dog. We certainly didn't need a quart of Bourbon whiskey when we were about to go on the platform in the auditorium of Baylor University. Baylor University is certainly not a very wet institution, I don't imagine.

"So, I couldn't think of any place to put it except to slip it right under where the bedspread was folded back up over the bolster—I just slipped it back under the bedspread.

"When the affair was over we were in a hurry, because the plane was ready to take off—we wanted to take off at a certain time, because we wanted to be in Washington at a certain time. Of course, there had been more speeches made than should have been made, and the time ran over what was scheduled. Everybody was rushing to get their hats. Oh, I had shown the President this bottle of whiskey and I said, 'What shall I do with it?'

" 'Well,' he said, 'put it out of sight. Don't let anybody see you carrying that thing around here—we'll be shot!'

"So, when we got back on the plane, it just occurred to me and I said, 'Boss, you know what I did with that quart of whiskey?'

"He said, 'No.'

"I said, 'I put it in the old President's bedstead.'

" 'My God,' he said, 'when they find that!—Of course, they may not find it for months, because that bedspread is only changed once a year probably.'

"It may still be there as far as I know."

HISTORY, BACKSTAGE: IRAN

Two weeks after getting home from Potsdam, Truman proposed a twenty-one-point program of domestic legislation for the postwar era. It was a blockbuster and ended his honeymoon with Congress. The reaction on Capitol Hill could be heard all over the country. According to the Republicans, this man, with whom they had expected to have little trouble, had gone berserk; all of a sudden he was trying to out-New Deal the New Deal. And from then on they resorted to every available means of discrediting Truman. The fight, which lasted as long as he was President, reached a high point in the congressional elections of 1946.

As predicted by the opinion polls (which already had shown a decline in his popularity of over fifty percentage points), the Democrats lost control of both houses of Congress. Such a defeat traditionally is considered a sure portent of defeat in the next presidential election. One believer in that axiom, Senator J. William Fulbright, of Arkansas, founder of the Fulbright Scholarships, went so far as to urge the President to resign and spare the country two more years of lame-duck leadership. Truman retorted that the Senator should have gone to a land-grant college and studied the Constitution.

Against this background it was remarkable that he was able to put through the two most important legislative proposals of his first term, the so-called Truman Doctrine and the Marshall Plan. Credit for their enactment went mostly to General Marshall, a towering supraparty figure, to Senator Arthur H. Vandenberg, of Michigan, the outstanding Republican authority on foreign affairs, and to Congress's obsessive fear of communism. It was a while before Truman himself was given credit for having manipulated these three factors to his advantage.

The Truman Doctrine came into being in response to notification from Clement Attlee, Churchill's successor as Prime Minister, that war-ravaged Britain no longer could afford to support Greece with economic and military aid. Since the Soviets had been putting intense pressure on Greece, as well as on Turkey and Iran, Attlee was saying in effect that the Mediterranean was ceasing to be a "British lake," as it had been called, and was about to become a Russian one.

The Truman Doctrine met the emergency with the promise of money, supplies and advisory personnel—possibly even more, if needed—not only for the immediately threatened countries but for any country that might find itself in comparable straits. So in a manner of speaking it was the official declaration of the Cold War, and it was carried further by the Marshall Plan, which offered economic rehabilitation to deserving, even *un*threatened Western European nations, and after that by the North Atlantic Treaty Organization, which offered outright military aid.

In 1953, when I first visited him in Independence, Truman told me that he had "called up" Stalin and bluffed him into withdrawing the Russian troops stationed in Iran. I could find no record of such a call, but the supposed facts I did find were so murky, so different in different versions, that it was hard to make out what did happen. In the *Memoirs*, the matter is left in the air; in other accounts it is presumably resolved by a voluntary pullback of Soviet forces, by a U.S. "ultimatum" and so on. The most rewarding reference to the subject I came across was by Dean Acheson in an interview with the editors [6] of Truman's *Memoirs*: . .

Question: One of the moot questions we have not been able to resolve

[6] William Hillman and David Noyes, a California advertising man.

is what the President said was an ultimatum concerning Iran, to Russia over Iran.

Acheson: You mean in 1945 and '46? I wasn't managing that, but I know about it because I was then Under-Secretary [of State]. I was familiar with the day-to-day part of it. He has used that expression [ultimatum] several times, but I never quite understood what he meant.

Q: He is supposed to have written a letter direct to Stalin, telling him to get his people out of there or we would move in.

A: If he did, I don't know anything about it.

Q: He is persistent in repeating this.

A: I should have thought that he may have had that a little twisted. As I remember the thing, it was quite clear that we were serious about this, but I don't think we ever got to the point of telling them we were going to move. I don't know what we had to move. We didn't have any troops. We had three divisions, I think, and that wouldn't have gone very far in there. If I had been Chief of Staff of the Army, I would have said, "Just a minute, boss. Have another look at this one."

I don't think we ever thought the Russians were going to move. The whole heart of the Russian idea during this period—and now, I think— the center of Russian interest, is the regime. That is more important to the people in the Kremlin than anything else. They are not going to do anything which will threaten the regime. A first-class, bang-up war with us would threaten that. Certainly at that time it would have. . . .

As reported in Chapter I, Truman mentioned to me two other subjects, besides Iran, which I wanted to find out more about. The others were: the men who, he said, had let him down (James Byrnes, Henry Wallace, Joseph Grew and Louis Johnson), and, second, the chance of the atomic bomb's destroying the world. These subjects also I pursued as well as I could after returning to Independence.

HISTORY, BACKSTAGE: FOUR MEN

Truman's troubles with his first Secretary of State, Byrnes, and his first Secretary of Commerce, Wallace, have been pretty well aired by now. In the words of Matt Connelly:

"Jim Byrnes was a very Machiavellian character, as Truman found out the hard way when he made him Secretary of State with his administration. Because Byrnes thought he was the real President. . . .

"When Truman was sworn in as President, Byrnes came in with a fully prepared speech that Byrnes and his boys had written for Truman. I read the thing. Now Byrnes just didn't give this to him as suggestions, he read it to him in his office. After he left, Truman showed me the speech. I said, 'Look, we've got ten guys in the Cabinet Room writing your speech, you can't use this, this is Jimmy Byrnes's, not Harry Truman's.' He threw it in the basket."

The differences between the new President and his Secretary of State came to a head in December 1945 when Byrnes, after a conference of foreign ministers in Moscow, prepared to make his report of the meeting in a nationwide radio address before making it to Truman. From then on, it was just a matter of time before he was replaced by General Marshall.[7]

As for Wallace, if the Secretary of State thought of himself as President, the Secretary of Commerce thought of himself as Secretary of State. He made the point most notably in a speech which he delivered in 1946 to a cheering crowd in Madison Square Garden, New York. Ad-libbing a bit, he detoured to the left of the down-the-middle text he had shown Truman and gave the administration the appearance of having two different foreign policies. After that, it was not long before he, too, was replaced.

Recorded while his *Memoirs* were in preparation, the following remarks offer the best explanation I could find of Truman's feelings about Joseph Grew:

"As I remember the thing, Leo Crowley [then Foreign Economic Administrator] and Joseph Grew, who was acting Secretary of State, came in [on May 8, 1945] and presented to me an Order on Lend-lease, which Crowley assured me was one that had been agreed to by Roosevelt, and it was time to sign it, and I signed it. It was a short document. I think we can dig up the Order.

"They immediately interpreted it literally and stopped all shipments to Russia particularly and other countries, too. But the vast majority of things were going to Russia on account of the fact that we were furnishing them immense quantities of food, clothing, arms and ammunition. They even went so far as to have some of the ships turn around and come back. That stirred up a hornet's nest in Russia. As soon as I saw what was happening, I immediately rescinded the Order. But the damage had been done, and Stalin at Potsdam would bring it up every chance he had, that we cut off Lend-lease while he was still getting ready to go to war in Japan.

"They made an agreement at Yalta they would be in the Japanese war three months after the Germans folded up. They stepped in just three days before it was over.

---

[7] On retiring in 1949 for reasons of health, General Marshall was succeeded by Dean Acheson, whom Truman called "one of the great Secretaries of State."

"I think Crowley and Grew put it over on me that morning. That taught me a lesson early in the game—that I should always know what was in those documents myself, personally, and I had to read all night some nights in order to do that."

Which places Grew in the doghouse but fails to decode Truman's cryptic characterization of him as "a ladies' man."

Last of the discordant quartet was Louis Johnson, who in Truman's second term succeeded the ailing James Forrestal as Secretary of Defense. One of the papers in Truman's personal file at the Library comments on Johnson's case:

"On General Pershing's birthday, September 12, 1950, I had to insist that the Secretary of Defense sign his letter of resignation—*and I had* to insist. . . . I am of the opinion that Potomac fever and a pathological condition are to blame for the fiasco at the end.

"Louis began to show an inordinate egotistical desire to run the whole government. He offended every member of the Cabinet. We never had a Cabinet meeting that he did not show plainly that he knew more about the problems of the Treasury, Commerce, Labor, Agriculture than did the Secretaries of those Departments. He played no favorites. . . .

"I tried to make it as easy on Johnson as circumstances would permit—but I had to force him to work in his own interest. He is the worst egomaniac I've ever come in contact with—and I've seen a lot."

HISTORY, BACKSTAGE: THE BOMB

Truman's fears that the Bomb might destroy the world had been quieted, he told me, by the scientists' assurance that there was only about a one-in-a-million chance of such a catastrophe.

The Bomb, of course, will remain a subject of controversy for years to come. At the time we talked about it, I could appreciate Truman's reasons for having approved its use: the huge saving in lives, both American and Japanese; the opportunity to end the war at a stroke and impose a kind of Pax Americana; the almost irresistible compulsion to employ a weapon on which the greatest scientists had collaborated and vast sums of money had secretly been spent, etc. But, leaving aside all that, together with the ultimate moral question, I still could not quite grasp how he, or anybody else, could have exploded the Bomb as long as there was any chance—any at all—of its ending the world.

The same thought, I later discovered, had exercised at least three of the scientists in the original atomic project. According to recently declassified documents, Drs. Eugene P. Wigner, Edward Teller and Emil J. Konopinsky made studies which convinced them that the Bomb would not, as they had feared, "ignite the atmosphere" and thus reduce the earth to the state of the moon.

Even after these findings, though, the question of the new weapon's potentiality remained moot enough to prompt Dr. Enrico Fermi, of the University of Chicago, to make book on it among the witnesses of the first nuclear explosion at Alamogordo. Less in earnest than in the hope of relieving the group's tension, Fermi asked his colleagues to bet on the degree of demolition each thought might result. Dr. J. Robert Oppenheimer, sometimes called "the father of the Bomb," is reported to have given one of the worst guesses: he greatly underestimated his baby's destructiveness.

Truman's latter-day attitude toward the mighty force he had unleashed can be gathered from a letter he wrote in 1957 to a University of Pennsylvania physicist, Norman Goldberg. It reads in part:

"Last weekend I had quite a discussion on the subject [of atomic energy] with one of our greatest authorities, Dr. Arthur H. Compton of Washington University in St. Louis. He was one of my original advisers, together with his brother, who was then head of the Massachusetts Institute of Technology, and he agrees with me. It is his opinion that all this talk is political, on the part of the scientists as well as the politicians.

"When Nobel invented TNT, he believed he had created a force to destroy the world, and his conscience hurt him so grievously that he set up his wonderful program of prizes for achievements in peaceful living. When artillery was first used in Italy, the artillerymen were hanged as inhuman beasts.

"Unfortunately a similar attitude towards our efforts to harness atomic energy seems to exist today, and I am very sorry about it. The objective is to find a way to make this tremendous release of energy useful and beneficial to all mankind, and it cannot be achieved without experimentation. . . ."

HISTORY, BACKSTAGE: 1948

When Truman became President, he scarcely knew Dean Acheson, who then was an assistant secretary of state. By the time he left office, Acheson, if not quite one of his innermost circle of friends, was close to it. Considered superficially, it was a curious rapproachement, for the two were far apart in background and training.

Acheson, the son of a Canadian distillery heiress and the Episcopal Bishop of Connecticut, was a product of the establishment; with his elegant clothes and language, his mustache, beetling brows and haughty air, he seemed, in fact, not only its product but its epitome. And Truman, during his early years in the capital, had been given little cause to cotton to such types; they had formed a sort of White House guard and had helped to make him feel like an outsider.

But beneath appearances Truman and Acheson had much in common. Both, for instance, were highly—indeed, romantically—principled. Acheson (as indicated in his already quoted letter about Truman's middle initial) was as sensitive to the old-fashioned concept of honor as Shakespeare's Hotspur was. Truman's view of the matter was less elevated: to him it was just a matter of doing what was right. But he was equally concerned about it and—as Acheson also was—about its attendant concepts of loyalty and courage, not as abstractions but as guides to everyday conduct.

These similarities might have gone undiscovered if it had not been for the fact that Secretary of State Byrnes and his successor, General Marshall, were away from Washington so much of the time. In their absence, Acheson, who had risen meanwhile to be Under Secretary, was the Department's anchorman and, as such, was in almost daily contact with the President. He and Truman collaborated on the Truman Doctrine and the Marshall Plan and, in the process, developed a genuine respect and liking for each other.

The quality of their friendship can be gauged from their correspondence, a sample of which, by Acheson, is given below. Excerpted from a series of letters he wrote in 1955 in response to a request for criticism of Truman's as yet unpublished *Memoirs*, these comments of his convey the spirit of the 1948 presidential election. As in Truman's senatorial race of 1940, nobody, it seemed, gave him a chance to win in '48 except Truman himself. One opinion poll became so convinced that Thomas E. Dewey, the Republican nominee, was going to be the next President of the United States that it actually stopped polling a month before election day. And Dewey for his part was so sure of the outcome that he gave the voters a glaring example of doing what Truman, in 351 "whistle stop" speeches, was charging the Republican Congress with having done, namely, nothing.

Here is Acheson's view of Truman's official version of his stirring victory:

"Chapter XIII. Here, Mr. President, I shall try your patience and good nature. The part up to and through page 277 should—I strongly urge—be wholly re-written. To me it does not ring true at all. The very opening words are all wrong—'If I had consulted my personal impulse . . . I should have made plans to leave the White House at the end of my first term.' This is not the fighting man that we all loved and love and who led the damnedest knock-down and drag-out in political history. The first thirteen pages do not impress the reader as Harry Truman speaking but as someone writing what Horatio Alger might have said under the circumstances. . . .

"The truth seems to be nearer this: your first term was brought about by the accident of death. You had never sought the job, you didn't want it. You hadn't been elected to it. But you had it and you tackled it as hard and conscientiously as you tackled everything. After a brief honeymoon, the tough boys wrote you off as of no account. They flouted your policies and began to reverse FDR's as hard as they could. They won the Congress in 1946. They overrode your vetoes. The press belittled you. The pollsters said you hadn't a chance. Many of your party went back on you. Reaction seemed to them to be in full swing. It was all personified in the 80th Congress.

"You have never run from a fight in your life. You knew damn well that the everyday American believed in what FDR and you stood for. Your Dutch, or Irish, or Missouri was up. You believed Americans would respond to fighting leadership and to the facts stated simply and powerfully. If the tough boys wanted a fight—and they didn't even believe there would be one—you would give them the golldarnedest fight they had ever had. You might get licked—you didn't think so but you might—but, if you did, the other guys would go to the Inaugural Ball with the biggest pair of shiners seen around these parts since Old Hickory put away his shillelagh.

"This sounds like you and like the truth. What has been written does not. It is too rational, too reluctant, too pious. The 'I never struck a blow except in defense of a woman' sort of thing. And the historical business on pages 268, 269 seems dragged in. You would have fought in '48 if no President ever had before.

"Much of the stuff on the later pages about the press, Congress, etc. is usable and good, but in a more fiery setting. However, the statement on page 277 that your trip [8] was not meant to be political; but non-partisan; you were not even a candidate, will seem to the reader insincere. Even in professional parlance, it squeaks by on the narrowest and most technical definition of 'political'. You were not on a lecture tour and you were running in the way in which at this stage a shrewd candidate had to run.

"Please put away the club you have out for me and rewrite these pages.

"If you do, then the latter part of the chapter about the impending splits

[8] Not the famous whistle-stop trip but a trial run for it in June 1948.

in the party by which you lost your right and left wings can be pointed up to their important and great significance.[9] They were infinitely more courageous decisions for a man who was going to pay the price for them and who wanted passionately to win, than they would have been for a retiring President or for a man who had no realization of their political consequences. It took cold nerve to do what you did, as you show later on by the fact that Ohio had the deciding votes. . . ."

The *Memoirs*, as published, reveal that this particular criticism of Acheson's had little effect. Other points of his had more. But, whether accepted or not, his forthright comments did not lessen the friendship between critic and author.

An afterthought of Truman's on the '48 election appears among his papers. It is headed: "Polls. Public Opinion Leadership."

"I wonder how far Moses would have gone if he'd taken a poll in Egypt?

"What would Jesus Christ have preached if he'd taken a poll?

"Where would the Reformation have gone if Martin Luther had taken a poll?

"It isn't polls or public opinion of the moment that counts.

"It's right and wrong and leadership—men with fortitude, honesty and a belief in the right that makes epochs in the history of the world."

As a final note on 1948, here is an exchange of letters between the newly-reelected President and the distinguished radio commentator H. V. Kaltenborn, who throughout election night had kept insisting that Truman's growing margin of victory soon would be wiped out. At dawn, when the margin had expanded to around two million votes, the same dogged voice could be heard saying that the contest would wind up in the House of Representatives, where it would be decided.

January 26, 1949

President Harry Truman
The White House
Washington, D.C.

Dear Mr. President:

I have just seen the newsreel which shows you delighting the Electoral College diners (and the moving picture audiences as well!) with your excellent imi-

---

[9] The right wing became the Dixiecrats under Governor Strom Thurmond of South Carolina, the left wing, the Progressive Party, under Henry A. Wallace.

tation of one H. V. Kaltenborn making false predictions on election night.

On Inauguration Day I told my radio audience how much we should all appreciate the generous and genial spirit with which you dealt with those who were dumbfounded by your victory. It showed, I said, that for the next four years we can all be human with Truman, as well as grateful for a leader with a sense of humor. Millions of Americans like you better as they have come to know you better.

May I wish for you a long continuance of that exuberant vitality which you displayed last week and the best of luck in implementing the magnificent program so effectively presented in your inaugural address.

Sincerely yours,
H. V. Kaltenborn

January 29, 1949

Mr. H. V. Kaltenborn
167 East 64th Street
New York 21, New York

Dear Mr. Kaltenborn:

I appreciate most highly your good letter of the twenty-sixth, and I assure you there was no malicious intent in the attempted take-off of your broadcast election night—it was merely for a good time and a little enjoyment after a terrific campaign.

You were very kind to write to me as you did.

Sincerely yours,
Harry S. Truman

HISTORY, BACKSTAGE: 1949

Assistant Press Secretary Eben Ayers was not the Truman Administration's only White House diarist. Harry Truman set the pace with a diary of his own, of which the following excerpts from the year 1949 are fairly typical:

Thursday, March 24

Mr. Churchill is coming to dinner. He came, brought me his Life of John Churchill, Duke of Marlborough. John's father was [named] Winston Churchill!

We had a very good time at dinner. General Marshall; Barkley, V.P.; Acheson, Sec. of State; C.J. Fred Vinson & Mrs. Vinson; the British Ambassador all made a contribution to the evening. (This Blair-Lee House is a handicap to such events.[10])

Mr. Churchill gave Bess his book on painting, which sold out the canvas and paint brush dealer in London!

The former P.M. looks old and yet he told me that in 1950 he'd be Prime Minister again and form either a Conservative or a Coalition Government! He may be as right as I was last year.

We had to go out and have pictures made on the "stoop". How we need the old building across the street, known as the White House. If Theodore Roosevelt and old man Coolidge had done as they should we wouldn't be out doors now!

Mr. Kim Meade White did a botch job in 1902 and the silent ? old man from Mass. did a worse one in 1927. It's hell. None of the Roosevelt tribe gave a damn about the official residence. They were all promoters for themselves, I'm sorry to say.

Sunday, March 27

Margie came home (not home, she came down to D.C.) on Wednesday so she could attend Winnie's dinner. Margie had a cold and couldn't work in N.Y. that is really why she came.

We, Margie & I, went for a walk at about 2 P.M. Had a grand time watching the reaction of the people. They were never sure that they were seeing what they really saw. All were smilingly polite but one damned sailor. He sat with his feet out in the way while we passed but his girl stood up, smiled & saluted.

Thursday, September 1

Press conference day. I start the proceedings off by an announcement on the loan for Mexican Oil Development. Then come questions which are many and varied. See report of conference.

Saturday, October 22

81st Congress quits after one hell of a session. The disappointed Republicans tried every strategy to ruin the session. Even the "good" ones joined the Dixiecrats of the Byrd, Ellender, McClelland stripe to defeat a program. They failed.

Saturday, October 29

Margaret sings in St. Louis tonight. Wish I could be present. It would spoil the performance were I to go. Bess is there and the V.P. and his lady. They have decided to make a go of it. I surely wish them well.

---

10 Mrs. Roosevelt had warned the Trumans that there were rats in the White House but not that the whole place was about to fall down. The fall began in 1948: a chandelier sagged and one of Margaret's pianos put a foot right through the floor. So in December the Trumans moved across the street to the Blair-Lee House, which usually was reserved for visiting dignitaries, and they remained there until the renovation of the White House was completed in 1952.

Talked to Bess and Margie in St. Louis. The concert was a wow—"hang-in' from the rafters," says Margie. She says the terrible *Post-Dispatch* (which hates me) and the old dyed in the wool conservative *Globe-Democrat* have been kind to her. Just read an old editorial from the *Globe-Democrat* today which came from Roosevelt's files of 1940. They'd decided that Missouri had gone to hell because I'd beaten the double-crosser Lloyd Stark for the nomination for the Senate! Stark had sent the piece to Roosevelt. It's hell how fate works. Stark wanted to be President—I didn't. Stark's buried politically bcause he is intellectually dishonest. I'm forced on the Democratic ticket by the man who thought Stark was tops—and I'm the President and in my own right.

It's hell on Margie but she's a good trouper!

Tuesday, November 1

I have another hell of a day. Look at my appointment list. It is only a sample of the whole year. Trying to make the 81st Congress perform is and has been worse than cussing the 80th. A President never loses prestige fighting Congress. And I can't fight my own Congress. There are some terrible chairmen in the 81st. But so far things have come out *fairly* well.

I've kissed and petted more consarned S.O.B. so-called Democrats and left wing Republicans than all the Presidents put together. I have very few people fighting my battles in Congress as I fought F.D.R.'s.

Had dinner by myself tonight. Worked in the Lee House office until dinner time. A butler came in very formally and said "Mr. President, dinner is served." I walk into the dining room in the Blair House, Barnett in tails and white tie pulls out my chair, pushes me up to the table. John in tails and white tie brings me a fruit cup, Barnett takes away the empty cup. John brings me asparagus, Barnett brings me carrots and beets. I have to eat alone and in silence in the candle-lit room—I ring—Barnett takes the plate and butter plates. John comes in with a napkin and silver crumb tray—there are no crumbs but John has to brush them off the table anyway. Barnett brings me a plate with a finger bowl and doily on it—and I remove the finger bowl and doily and John puts a glass saucer and a little bowl on the plate. Barnett brings me some chocolate custard. John brings me a demitasse (at home a little cup of coffee—about two good gulps) and my dinner is over. I take a hand bath in the finger bowl and go back to work.

What a life!

HISTORY, BACKSTAGE: 1950

As he observed in the previously quoted farewell address, the worst of Truman's problems was the Korean War. What made it so, he used to say, was that it wasn't just a matter of one country vs. another country; it was a matter of a lot of countries on the American side acting under the aegis of the United Nations, the majority in agreement but none enthusiastically and some in dissent. Getting things done in those conditions required great firmness and great tact.

The division of Korea (the name means "land of the morning calm") between the Russian-occupied north and the U.S.-occupied south was an awkward consequence of then Secretary of State Byrnes's negotiating at the 1945 Conference of Foreign Ministers. Byrnes agreed to a joint Soviet-U.S. Commission to establish a provisional Korean government until a more lasting government could be formed. But he failed to define exactly what the provisional one was to be like. When the UN dispatched a temporary commission to supervise free Korean elections, the Russians refused to let it into their territory. Then they dropped an iron curtain along the 38th Parallel.

In June 1950, Truman was spending a weekend in Independence when he got a telephone call from Secretary of State Dean Acheson, notifying him that the North Koreans had invaded the south. There was a bit of luck here at the start: the Russians had walked out of the UN Security Council in protest over its refusal to allow the seating of Red China. So when a Security Council meeting was called to consider the Korean situation, the Soviets were absent.

But it was a tricky course Truman was embarked on, with the Republicans out to shoot him down, with Chiang Kai-shek trying to use the occasion to recoup his loss of mainland China to the Communists and with General MacArthur's grandiose ambitions. Also there were the big military gambles, in particular MacArthur's Inchon landing plan, which Truman approved even though it was about as risky a stratagem as Hannibal's crossing of the Alps.

"I'd been up in northwest Missouri on some bar activities," Rufus Burrus said, "and on the way back I stopped, with my son along with me, to see Mr. Truman. I said, 'Good to see you. I'm going to Washington for the meeting of the Reserve Officers Association. By the way, if you're going back, I'd like to deadhead with you.' He said, 'Sure.' Turned to his aide and said, 'Put Burrus on the manifest.'

"He was going Monday. So Sunday I went to church. Mrs. Burrus wasn't feeling well and she didn't go; my son and I went and came back home. She said, 'Mr. Truman's aide's been trying to get you. They're going to leave this afternoon at 1:30, and they want you to be at the airport today instead of tomorrow.' [11]

[11] Dean Acheson's call came in Saturday night, June 24.

"So I got my things together and got over to the airport and Mr. Truman was there and the plane was there, but it didn't have all its crew, just Rose [Conway], Fred Wallace [Bess's brother] and a few others. Then, later, in the plane, with Snyder, he had to tell him what was transpiring, what looked like was going to have to be done. Said the United Nations were going to have to make a resolution or something that would call upon the North Koreans to stop, desist their invasion. If they didn't, they'd have to have a police action to put it to an end.

Q: He used that expression, police action?

"Police action, that's what he used. John Snyder understood it, John has verified it. He [Truman] said, 'We're going to have a conference with the Chiefs of Staff, the Cabinet and others, we're going to have a buffet supper. Of course, you can't be at that, you and Fred, you'll be upstairs, but we'll get you some supper, too. We'll see how good a supper this crew can get on short notice.' Well, we got there and they had a good supper fixed up for us.

"Later that evening, about nine o'clock, after they'd all left, he came upstairs, we had agreed we were going to take a walk next morning and have a swim. He said, 'You'll have to take a rain check on the swim and walk, because I'm going to have to get that work done in the morning, so I won't have a chance to do that.'

"Next morning I got up and came downstairs and there he was at the writing table, he had his big yellow tablet and several pages he'd written on it. His handwriting is the most easily read. He said, 'Maybe you'd like to read this.' There was his speech to the joint session of Congress. I said, 'Yes.' And I'm of the firm conviction that that was the way it was finally written, I don't think it had much change in it of any kind. . . . Anyway, that morning I read it and we had breakfast. Then I went on my way down to the Mayflower Hotel."

Q: He wrote this before breakfast?

"Before breakfast. He'd finished it, he was looking at the newspapers when I saw him. He'd been up much earlier. I got up a little after six. So I tell people maybe the President and the Chief Justice and other people have ghost writers to write things for them, but I can tell you one document I know was written by him. That was what he did. No ghost writer. You remember, he appeared before the joint session, he was applauded by the newspapers everywhere as to the course of action he was taking, and then as the thing wore on they called it 'Truman's war.' 'Twasn't any more his war than it was my war or anyone else's.

"The next morning, when he came by to pick me up [at the hotel] and take a walk, why we were walking around in the neighborhood, one of the Secret Service men came up and said, 'Mr. President, there's a telephone call from Averell Harriman.' 'Oh,' he said, 'I don't want to take it at one of these places in the street. Tell him I'll cut the walk short and go down and get it at the swimming pool.'

"So we cut around some of the corners that he knew and we got down to the swimming pool and I got my swimming suit on and he got his. Somebody wanted him on the telephone. It was Harriman. He said, 'Averell, close station, march orders. I've got more important things for you to do back here at home.' That's an artillery phrase: Close station, march orders. Harriman later said, 'That's right, that's what he said.' Harriman was in Paris, I think. Any rate, he came on back.

"Truman then said, 'Well, better take our swim, you better get your swim.' Then he said, 'There's a corpsman over there, he is paid and instructed to take me on that table and beat the hell out of me.' "

Q: Did Mr. Truman ever talk to you about General MacArthur?

"Yes, well, he told me that he went across the country, halfway across the world to see him because MacArthur was just too damn busy to come see his Commander in Chief. He wanted MacArthur to come back here, and MacArthur always was too busy. So he said, 'All right, I'll meet you halfway at Wake Island.' So he did. He said, 'I wanted him to be informed exactly why he needed to stop short of the Yalu River, and why we couldn't involve ourselves in anything except to stop at that point. Because we'd lose our allies, we'd lose the help of the United Nations, we'd be in the wrong place for a conflict—it was too far away, it would be too costly in men and munitions. It would be a horrible thing to get stuck with, and I wanted him to understand and know it. And I thought that was the end of it.' "

It was the beginning of it. In the Wake Island meeting, MacArthur, a picture of reasonableness, assured Truman that the Korean War was won, that Red China was in no position to cause trouble and that he would soon be able to release a division for service in Europe.

From there on events moved swiftly:

October 16 (the day after the Wake conference): Chinese troops flouted MacArthur's prediction by crossing the Yalu River into North Korea, heading south.

November 1: American regiment dispersed in first engagement with Chinese, en masse.

November 6–7: MacArthur asked for, and was denied, permission to bomb Yalu River bridges and strike at Chinese in their lair.

Uproar over Korea cost Democrats a parcel of Senate and House seats in the election.

It is 6 A.M., the year 1953, on a summer morning in Independence, Missouri, when Harry Truman, citizen, who has been up for an hour, goes outside for the morning paper. "That newsboy has good aim. I usually find the newspaper fairly easily, but sometimes it winds up in the bushes. A good throw lands it on the front steps."

Leaving the house was never easy. Every morning he paused to accommodate the amateur photographers and autograph hunters. Truman was not entirely happy about the iron fence with its electronically controlled gate. It had been installed in 1947 by the government to provide security that Truman never thought he needed.

In a cool shady lane near the Truman home the former President stops to speak to an early-rising neighbor who was prun- ing the trees around his home. No one ever caught Truman outside in an under- shirt at this or any other hour.

Truman's traditional summer garb was a jaunty Panama hat, a white shirt, a light-blue medium-width tie, blue striped handkerchief, double-breasted navy-blue suit and black-and-white shoes. Asked why he always wore a tie and jacket and carried his ever-present walking cane, he replied, "I feel a lot more comfortable. I never know who I'm likely to meet, so I try to be prepared."

The ex-President politely tips his hat and says good morning to two flustered but pleased young women on their way to work.

"Each morning walk is different," said Truman. On this particular morning walk when Truman stops to speak to a youngster, a storekeeper with a movie camera steps out of his doorway and begins filming the scene. (Note that Truman has changed ties and shoes and walking cane.)

In the early stages of Truman's morning walk the streets of Independence are quiet and deserted. He once estimated that he took two steps per second, 120 per minute, or about 10,000 steps in the hour-and-a-half walk. When he first saw this photograph he said, "I didn't even know the sign was there—but it's good advice."

"It just isn't possible for me to sleep late. There are always people waiting at the front gate when I leave for my walk and others there when I return. I think I'd miss them, though, if no one showed up." (While this visitor to Independence is chatting with the ex-President, her husband is photographing them.)

The early-morning sun throws long shadows across the quiet street as Truman is joined by author Charles Robbins. Trying to keep out of sight and to keep up with Harry Truman—who never slowed down —I (photographer Bradley Smith) had an athletic morning.

Back home and comfortable on the much-used screened porch, Truman checks out one paper's coverage of news events against the others. He firmly believed that news is likely to be slanted and that it is important to read several papers.

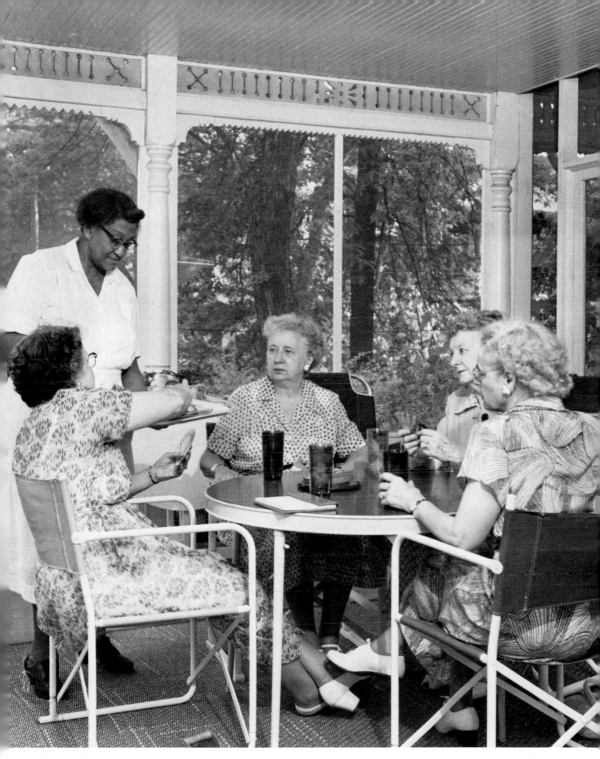

Vietta Garr, housekeeper and cook for the Trumans, serves a choice of ginger ale or Coca-Cola at Mrs. Truman's afternoon canasta game. She became part of the Truman household in 1926, went to the White House with them and returned with them when the Trumans came home to stay in Independence. These same Independence friends played canasta with Bess Truman a couple of times a month. Mrs. Truman laughed and joked during this game—which she and her partner won.

"These parking meters are too complicated: I can never tell where to push the
nickel in," Truman complained, after trying once and dropping his nickel before he finally succeeded.

アメリカ合衆國.
元大統領
トルーマン閣下

Independence, Missouri,
U.S.A
Sr. Harry Truman

Mail came in from all over the world for Harry Truman, and he and Rose Conway answered all of it. During his first two weeks back in Independence he received more than 70,000 pieces of mail.

"I'm always in a hurry to see the mail." He did not consider it a chore to carry his canvas mailbag to the post office. "It's easy enough going in, but I often have to get help to carry it out to the car."

The Jackson County Courthouse in Independence contained the office of Judge Harry Truman. He was proud of his part in redesigning this courthouse in 1931, and he especially liked the equestrian statue of General Andrew Jackson near the entrance.

Here the camera has caught the simplicity, warmth and sincerity of a typical Truman discussion. He was speaking of his plans for the Truman Library to be built in Independence and presented to the people of the United States.

Visiting his sister Mary Jane, Truman watched as she showed off the ball-playing ability of her dog Barkley, named after Truman's former Vice-President. When the dog jumped, Truman said, "That dog is almost as tall as I am—and that's not saying much."

She remembered her Latin and math pupil Harry very well indeed. "He was a good student—gave me no trouble," said the ex-President's former schoolteacher Miss Ardelia Hardin. She gave up teaching to marry the high school principal, W. L. C. Palmer.

Two years younger than Harry, his brother Vivian stayed on the farm when Harry went into politics. On a visit to Vivian's farm, Harry reminisced and watched the antics of an unusual combination—a friendly dog and cat—while Vivian's wife Luella served lemonade.

On the Grandview farm the ex-President, his namesake (Vivian's son, Harry) and Harry's daughter, Wanda Lee, climbed up onto the fence to see the new pinto foal. "It reminds me of my first horse, a Shetland pony," said Truman.

Horses often played a part in the life of
**Harry S. Truman. He was given a Shet-
land pony at the age of four. He rode regularly on the farm and later, as a captain**
in the U.S. Army Artillery, rode a horse
in the September 1918 Argonne offensive.
He seemed very happy to be mounted on
one again.

Leaving the Grandview farm, Truman shook hands and said goodbye to "Tiny" Lee Sage, who worked on the farm with Vivian. "He is as bighearted as he is big," said Truman. Then, commenting on this unusual formality, "Everyone wants to shake my hand—you'd think I was still President."

With portraits of daughter Margaret on his left and wife Bess behind him, the former President often settled down with a book before (and frequently after) dinner. Favorite subjects: history, biography and government. Bess especially liked mysteries—and Harry read one occasionally.

Harry Truman had studied and played the piano since he was seven. Most people thought "The Missouri Waltz" was his only number, but he read music, loved Mozart and Chopin. The music on the piano is "Ave Maria"; he bought the piano for Margaret on her eighth birthday. One contemporary political cartoon showing the President at the piano was captioned, "Don't shoot the piano player—he's doing the best he can!"

Surrounded by the furniture inherited and
accumulated during their marriage, Bess
and Harry Truman read in their comfort-

able living room. They were usually in bed
by 10:30 P.M. The top magazine on the
coffee table is the *Atlantic Monthly*.

In front of the house at 219 N. Delaware Street in Independence stand Harry S. Truman—thirty-third President of the United States—and Bess Wallace Truman, his wife. When the picture was taken in 1953, Bess was sixty-eight, Harry sixty-nine. Except for the years when Truman was Senator and President, they spent their married life in this house built by Mrs. Truman's grandfather in 1867.

November 26: MacArthur ominously reported his forces outnumbered by Chinese army, a quarter million strong.

November 28: Another charged report from MacArthur, again demanding permission to enlarge the war, again denied.

November 30: Rumors that atom bombs were to be used against Chinese. Prime Minister Attlee, of Britain, rushed to Washington for consultations.

December 5: Press Secretary Charles Ross died at his desk. Not informed of the tragedy, Margaret Truman gave concert in Washington, incurred random criticism for poor taste, particular criticism from *Washington Post* for quality of performance. Truman, tried to the limit, lashed back at *Post* music critic. . . .

In the early months of the new year, 1951, the political and military situations improved. In March, Truman was planning to put out a peace feeler to the Chinese. Notified of it, MacArthur issued a statement of his own which turned the feeler into a goad. He followed up with a letter to Representative Joseph Martin, Republican minority leader, and Martin read it aloud in the House; it was a proposal to forestall World War III in Europe by starting it right there and then, in the Far East. With that, Truman finally set in motion the machinery to oust MacArthur, and the ousting was announced on April 11.

All hell broke loose. Senator Joseph McCarthy, of Wisconsin, stopped hunting closet communists in the State department long enough to charge that Truman had acted while drunk. Senator Richard Nixon called for MacArthur's reinstatement. Senator William Jenner called for Truman's impeachment. Representative Joseph Martin and other Republican leaders contrived to invite MacArthur to come home and address a joint session of Congress.

MacArthur accepted the invitation and was wildly greeted. In Washington, with the whole country stopping work to listen in on the radio, he told the joint congressional session, "Old soldiers never die, they just fade away."

It looked as though the Democrats were the ones about to fade away. But Truman kept his head, saying, "He hasn't got any real support. It'll blow over." And he was right. Indeed, according to Colonel Burrus, Truman himself gave it a modest nudge toward oblivion:

"Well, I've learned that he [MacArthur] was lent an aircraft, he'd asked permission to use it [to fly around, giving speeches]. And I've learned that Mr. Truman said, 'Yes, let him use the aircraft, let him have it, but don't service it. Let him wear it out.' It got to be dangerous for him after thirty days.

"Mr. Truman knew that he couldn't treat him like an ordinary disobedient officer, you had to treat him with deference. He did respect his ability. I've been told by some that MacArthur afterwards realized that he'd made a mistake and shouldn't have done what he did; he was rather penitent about it. . . ."

Harry Vaughan's comments on Generalissimo Stalin appeared early in this chapter, so an appropriate way to end it may be with a comment of Eddie McKim's on another Generalissimo, MacArthur. During a trip to Paris in September 1945, McKim met General George C. Patton. While they were talking, one of the General's entourage showed them a Paris paper with a headline announcing that MacArthur had just been named Supreme Commander for the Allied Powers in Japan.

"Georgie Patton," McKim says, "had a high, squeaky voice, and he said, 'Look at that, look at that! Well, I'll say this, there's one S.O.B. who'll show Hirohito how to be an Emperor!' And he did!"

XI

Independence Again

IF YOU ARE IN A CAR APPROACHING INDEPENDENCE FROM THE EAST ON Interstate 70, as I was, the first indication that you are nearing your destination is a roadside sign of modest size that reads, "Sauna Baths. Massage." It has a picture of a pretty girl, saying, "Visit me," and the address is Truman Road.

The sign is a portent of what lies ahead as you turn off the highway at Noland Road (named after Ethel Noland's family) into a jumble of fast-food joints, garages, automobile showrooms, motels, chain stores, all looking about as permanent as an ice cream cone on a hot day.

I asked Colonel Burrus what Truman had thought of the changes that, in one generation, have transformed Independence from another Athens into another suburb.

"He didn't have a chance to see too much of what's happened up on the Square," the Colonel replied, "because after that happened he was more or less confined to home. But what little he saw—it hurt him to know that they were trying to make the Square something which it was not. The Square was the meeting place, and the courthouse was the center of activity of Independence. When they put up those shopping centers around, he didn't think that was the best thing that could happen to us.

"Mrs. Truman was the most outspoken about those things, even today. It just offends her what they've done to the town up here. The first thing people used to do when they'd come here would be to go around the Square first in one direction and then the opposite direction. We used to call it winding the clock. We'd come to town and before we'd leave we'd wind the clock on the Square.

"Then they came along and closed up the east side and then the west side so you can't get through, and they put up those barriers on the north and south side and made a one-way street out of it. It would have just broken his heart.

"He was greatly pleased to make this Georgian type architecture out of this courthouse—and to see what they've done to it, making it look bizarre! And over there across the street in front of where his statue is they had the temerity to attempt to put in a platform where they had people playing hard rock music and dancing and all that kind of thing.

"I went over there and I chided them and I tried to talk to them on the outside and we had to get rough and mean on the inside. And Mrs. Truman said, 'You tell them I don't want that!' And I said, 'I'll tell them!'

"But they still went ahead. They put up a platform temporarily across the street over there, had it for two or three days. There's no reason in the world to make that kind of place out of it. I said, 'You want to put something on the Square, put it on the west side or the north side, but don't put it in front of his office, in front of his statue.'

"Another thing about our town, there's a hundred and twenty thousand people here now, and I don't suppose more than five thousand of us have been here more than twenty years. These people come in, they haven't the sense of history or the understanding to know what our town is. They think they made the town."

Q: When I was here, Mr. Truman drove me down to Grandview, and at that time that was where he wanted to put the Library.

"Well, the reason why I think he changed his mind from out there was it wasn't really the place, it wasn't the county seat, it wasn't a place where people would have easy access and it was away from his home. He wanted it close by his home.

"That's the reason he looked around the town here and finally—this was a park that had been purchased by a woman whose husband had been a circuit judge. Slover had been his name and Mrs. Slover had given $10,000, and they bought that land for Slover Park. She had given the land to the town. And Mr. Truman, exercising his options for a place to put it [the Library], had contact with our Mayor, Tom Weatherford. Weatherford thought that that would be a good place to have it out there.

"And it was a good place, except that they needed more ground and higher ground. The ground in the park was on the west side, which sloped down. Where the Library is actually located is another block they bought and all the houses on it; they paid $100,000 and got that property assembled, moved the houses off and used that as the location for the Library. . . ."

Frances Myers's family knew the Trumans; for a while they had a farm adjoining the Truman farm in Grandview. In 1951, after working as a secretary in the Pentagon, Miss Myers transferred to the White House at the invitation of Rose Conway, whose backup secretary she became in the President's office. I had hoped to find out something about Truman's later days from Rose, whom I'd got to know in 1953. I did call on her, but she was too ill and frail to be of much help.

So I turned to Frances, who had been married and widowed since I'd last seen her and now was living in a huge retirement "village" on the outskirts of Kansas City. She is a handsome woman in the Valkyrian mold. Everything about her looked brand-new: hairdo, clothes, furniture, apartment, indeed, the whole development.

"When we came back here in 1953," she said, "we had that office you saw in the Federal Reserve Bank Building—Mr. Truman and Rose and I—and the policeman the city assigned to us. We moved to the Library about a month before it was dedicated, in July 1957.

"Mr. Truman came to work mostly every weekday and Saturday mornings, too, although Rose and I didn't come in then except when there was something unusual. He came in alone on Saturdays. But he kept regular office hours at the Library until 1969. He stayed home after that; he was beginning to fail a little. But he still worked. He'd have Rose come over to the house with the mail and take his letters and do whatever else needed to be done. I went a few times. . . ."

Truman's mail, she said, used to average around forty letters a day. To her astonishment, people often would enclose unsolicited sums of money. Unless they specified that it was to go to the Library or the Democratic National Committee, it always would be returned to them with thanks.

Once, she recalled, a veterans group wrote that they had no flag; would Mr. Truman please send them one? Truman was very upset about it. Then he learned that this group was connected with others, which no doubt would hear of his sending the first a flag and ask the same favor, so he refused the request. But he continued to be disturbed at the thought of a group of flagless veterans.

While she was talking, I thought about her way of coping with advancing age and Truman's. With him it had been business as usual, life as usual; here, it was a gentle slide to the bottom.

It had taken me twenty minutes of driving through the village's maze of streets to find her place, a one-story building made up of two or three apartments. Besides this kind of multiple unit, the development contained individual houses, high-rise apartment buildings, administration buildings, etc. In the hundreds. An unnatural stillness lay over everything, contributed to by the paucity of children. Nor was much life evident in the houses. Driving along, I had the feeling that people were just sitting inside there, waiting.

Truman's spinster sister, Mary Jane, aged eighty-six, shuddered when I mentioned Frances Myers's retirement village. She said she wouldn't think of living in a place like that. Mary Jane's home is a three-bedroom bungalow in Grandview, a block from the town's main street. The day before calling on her, I had talked to a man who had known the Trumans for over forty years. I'd heard that she hadn't been well and was wondering if it would be all right to try to see her.

"Why don't you call her up?" he asked. "If she doesn't want you to come, she'll say so. Miss Mary always speaks her mind."

He continued, "She had a fall a while ago, but the neighbors came and got her up. She won't let anybody live with her. She's that kind of person. She wants to be alone, and they have to leave her alone. She was sick for a time. They had her in the hospital on various occasions and when she went home they had to have somebody be with her. She didn't like that, so they sent her to a nursing home. But she got so disenchanted there that she was willing to have somebody come to the house. 'Well, this won't last long,' she said to the woman. 'I'm going to make you go home.' And she finally did and stayed on by herself. She uses a walker, but she does fall once in a while." [1]

So I telephoned Miss Mary, whom Truman had introduced me to in 1953, and when I said I wanted to show her some pictures of her brother she told me to come ahead.

It was raining the morning I arrived at her house, which is small and white, with a screened-in porch. I rang the bell beside the porch door and stood there in the rain until a woman's voice said testily, "Well, why don't you come in? I can't come down to you. I've got this walker."

She was barely visible in the gloom, a small figure, posed in the frame of an inner doorway. As I crossed the porch, she turned and hobbled into a shadowy living room, with a standing lamp on. I wouldn't have recognized her. The angular, competent-looking woman I remembered had

---

[1] I regret not being able to give this man's name. At first he was willing to let it be used. Then he asked to see a transcript of his remarks. After I had shown him one, he told me I could print what he'd said but only anonymously. His subsequent contributions are attributed to Anon.

blossomed into a rosy-cheeked, white-haired fairy godmother, whose blue eyes twinkled at me behind her spectacles. I got out the handbound book of Bradley Smith's 1953 photographs and held it in my lap, sitting beside her under the lamp while she slowly turned the pages. She brooded over each photograph as raptly as a child would have done.

"Harry always did take a good picture," she kept saying. "Harry always did take a good picture. . . ."

When we had finished with the book and she had given me her opinion of retirement villages, she said that with the help of the walker she could get around well enough to do a lot of her own chores, including the cooking. Of course, Vivian's [2] sons, Fred and J.C., and their wives helped with the marketing, as did the neighbors, who would drop in now and then to see how she was.

Then she started talking about the Secret Service men who had been assigned to them after a couple of Puerto Rican nationalists had tried to assassinate Harry in Blair House.[3]

"There were three Secret Service men and one of them used to—they were all wonderful, I still get Christmas cards from two of them—but one of them used to lift Mama up and change her position when she felt tired. That was when she couldn't get around—after her fall. She just thought he was the greatest thing, he was so gentle. . . ."

And she mentioned an incident which apparently had played a part in bringing in the Secret Service men and also illuminated her mother's peculiar innocence and rectitude. While taking a bath one day, she had heard voices in the living room, where she had left her mother alone. She couldn't imagine who the visitor could be; so she finished her bath, threw on some clothes and hurried out. There was a strange woman sitting there, and in a minute or two it dawned on her that this woman was mentally disturbed. Mary Jane got rid of her as quickly as she could. The moment the door closed, her mother said, "Why, Mary Jane, that wasn't like you at all! You're usually so polite and nice! You weren't very polite to that woman!"

"But Mama, she was a little off mentally—that's why I did it!"

Martha Ellen remained disapproving; just because the poor woman might have been a little off, she felt, was no reason to be rude to her.

In a talk with Fred Truman the preceding week, I'd learned that eleven acres of the Truman farm, including the house, had not gone with the

[2] Vivian Truman died in 1968. His eldest son, J.C., lives in Independence; the next, Fred, not far from Grandview; and the two youngest, with wives, children and their mother, on a Kansas farm. His daughter, a lawyer, married to another lawyer, also lives in Kansas.
[3] November 1950. Truman escaped injury, but one attacker and a guard were killed.

wind; they still were owned by Vivian's two youngest sons and their mother. Now, as I was leaving, Miss Mary surprised me with a reference to "the tenants living there." I had noticed signs in the Truman Corners shopping center, directing the public to "The Truman Home," and had supposed that the place was being maintained by the municipality or state as a memorial. To have people living in it seemed as odd as to have tenants in Grant's Tomb. But Miss Mary just said they paid their rent and ushered me out.

Question: Except for diphtheria when he was a kid, and his eye trouble, Mr. Truman seems to have enjoyed splendid health until after I saw him in 1953. The next year he had a gall bladder operation, which he got over before anybody thought he would. But toward the end, around 1970, he seems to have deteriorated rapidly—is that correct?

Anon.: He was old, eighty-six in 1970. His arteries weren't what they were. It crept up on him. He just slowed down, had some arthritis, lost weight.

Q: How about mentally?

A: He was slower to think and act, but he still had that happy attitude of his.

Q: And Mrs. Truman? [4]

A: She's been sick, but she's still as alert as can be. She was in the hospital last spring. Had a fall. The doctor came out to see her. She wasn't going to listen to him and go to the hospital. Said she wasn't hurt, she was all right. But next morning she began to feel pain and was willing to go. It was good she did because they got a chance to check her medications, what she needed to have done for her arthritis and all. They persuaded her to use a walker. She gets around that way now, and she uses a hearing aid. But she keeps up with everything just like she always did—

Q: Does she still read mystery stories?

A: Oh, my, yes, she's got a whole stack of them. Follows the sport news, baseball and basketball—she's been interested in that since she was a girl. But lots of times she doesn't feel like seeing people. I'll be going to see her, and she'll call and say, "Don't feel very good. Something has kind of disturbed me. I think I better not have you come by today." I'll ask if there's anything I can do for her, and she'll say, "No, I'll be all right. . . ."

She did something a little unusual for her two weeks ago. Had Mrs. Mondale call on her—the Vice-President's wife, she was here to see the

---

[4] Mrs. Truman was ninety-two in 1977.

Library. They had a nice visit, and Mrs. Truman said she was a very gracious woman. But most times she doesn't like to have people come to see her.

Q: Does a Secret Service man stay there with her?

A: They have a bungalow across the street, the Secret Service. They have surveillance equipment there, round the Truman house. Cameras. They can tell everything that goes on.

Q: Does anybody stay in with her?

A: In the daytime she has these servants, women. They've been with her quite a while, two of them have. The Secret Service men, they come over and they also stay in the house at night, they're on duty. They're not sleeping there, they're just around the house, watching. Then she has a yard man and a house man, who comes in—

Q: Some people were telling me they saw the Secret Service car parked in front of a beauty parlor near the Square.

A: That's where she goes to the beauty shop.

Q: And Mrs. Truman was inside; they could see her through the doorway, under a dryer.

A: They take her there and bring her back, the Secret Service.

Q: What does she do otherwise?

A: Oh, my, she has a telephone by her side. She telephones, talks to people. Talks to Margaret in New York every day or two. Most usually Margaret makes the call, because she knows her mother's there. And she gets periodicals, news magazines, *The New York Times*—Margaret's husband is with *The New York Times,* you know, and she keeps track of that and the local papers. She doesn't watch much television, except for sports. She'd rather read and know what it is that way.

Q: Does she still belong to a bridge club—or canasta club? It was canasta when I was here.

A: Well, I guess they have a bridge club, but they don't play cards. They come by and see her. They call, and she arranges for them to come in.

Q: Are any of her brothers still alive?

A: No, she has some in-laws, some cousins and nieces, but she's the last of the family—Wallaces.

Often in the evening or at night I'd drive past 219 North Delaware Street on the way to the place where I was staying and never see a light or any sign of life. Back in 1953, despite the iron fence which Herbert Hoover had advised Truman to put up for protection, the house had seemed to be integrated into the neighborhood. Now it was standing apart, already starting to look like a monument.

Should I try to invade the monument? The question kept recurring to me all through my stay in Independence. On the negative side, there were Mrs. Truman's age, her health and reclusiveness, and the failure of anyone really close to her to offer to usher me into her presence. If she should remember me after a quarter of a century, after all the journalists who had badgered her in the meantime, it would be miraculous; if not, an embarrassment. Besides, what could I say in a few minutes to justify the intrusion? ("Would you be kind enough to bring me up to date on your life?" "Why, of course, I've just been waiting for somebody to ask me that.")

Finally, on my last afternoon in town, October 9, I decided to do as I'd done with Miss Mary—call her up. A couple of anecdotes figured in this decision. The night before, Mrs. Carvin [5] had told me that there was a man down the street who by arrangement with the Trumans had been shooting the pigeons off their house for years—an odd kind of job but evidently a fact. He recently had telephoned Mrs. Truman to say he couldn't do it any more, he was getting too old. "Too old!" she exclaimed. "You don't know the half of it!"

The other anecdote was presented to me by the Andrew Grays [6] when I went over to their place in Topeka, Kansas, for dinner. Mr. Gray had given his wife, Georgia, a necklace with a bauble on it of Venetian glass, very pretty. Not long afterward they called on Mrs. Truman and he gave *her* a necklace exactly like the other, saying jokingly that he didn't think Georgia would like this because he'd told her that her necklace was for his best girl. "Well," said Mrs. Truman, "she can be your best girl in Kansas and I'll be your best girl in Missouri."

Neither story suggested that Mrs. Truman was having any trouble holding up her end of a conversation.

So I telephoned her. She answered, and after stumbling around trying to identify myself, I wound up saying lamely that I was leaving the next day and would like to see her for a minute or two, for auld lang syne.

"I'm sorry," she said. "I can't see anybody today. I'm not feeling well."

There was some kind of background noise. I apologized for disturbing her and, hanging up, wondered if the Secret Service had her phone bugged, maybe that accounted for the noise. Then I hit on a better explanation:

[5] A widow in her seventies, also using a walker, Mrs. Grace Carvin is one of that peerless breed of elderly women that seems to be indigenous to western Missouri. She has turned her North Delaware Street home into a sort of dormitory for Truman researchers. While I was there her friends were trying to persuade her to sell the house and move to Frances Myers's retirement village, and she was standing them off valiantly.

[6] Georgia Gray, formerly Georgia Neese Clark, was appointed Treasurer of the United States by Truman, the first woman to hold the post.

That afternoon the Kansas City Royals and the New York Yankees were having a pre-World Series playoff game in the Royals' stadium. I bet she was watching them on television or listening on the radio, and as between that and talking to some nosy journalist there just was no choice at all.

The last of this series of interviews was with John Snyder. Before leaving Independence, I gathered from talking to people and from the available literature that he had been the White House conservative, a counterweight to the liberals. The role could not have been an easy one since it had pitted him against the likes of Henry Wallace, Clark Clifford, Sam Rosenman and other New Dealers, not to mention Truman himself on occasion. To have come through as well as he had must have taken a lot of discretion, a quality suggested also by the sealing of most of the material he has contributed to the Library and the blandness of what has been left open. So in arranging to see him in Washington (where at eighty-three he was chairman and moving spirit of the Harry S. Truman Scholarship Foundation), I was more curious to meet the last articulate member of the four musketeers of Fort Riley than hopeful of uncovering anything new.

The Harry S. Truman Scholarship Foundation has its headquarters in an attractive townhouse a few stones' throws from the White House. On the brilliant fall afternoon I arrived there, the place was wrapped in a hush, almost a spell, which a woman receptionist, all by herself in a front room, and Snyder, also alone at a big desk in the second-floor rear room, seemed loath to break. With his back to the windows, immobile, a plump ageless man with a high forehead, dark hair and what used to be called horn-rimmed glasses, through which he regards you unblinkingly, he called up memories of the figures of minor deities in Japanese wayside shrines.

Hoping to make as much of the occasion as possible, I had brought along a tape recorder, which he politely asked me not to use, so I began scribbling in a memorandum book already pretty full of addresses, notes, etc. As a result, the most coherent direct quotes of his I have are from a transcript he gave me of some recent remarks he'd made to a Senate committee which was passing on his nomination as a foundation trustee.

"The Harry S. Truman Scholarship program," he told the Senators, "was the outcome of a desire on the part of Senator Stuart Symington of Missouri and me to develop an appropriately prestigious congressional memorial to our late great President, Harry S. Truman. . . .

"President Truman and I met in 1920 at an officers' training camp at Fort Riley, Kansas. Both of us had served as field artillery officers in World War I—he as a battery commander in the 35th Division, and I as a brigade operations officer of the 57th field artillery brigade of the 32nd Division.

"After the war, both of us had been invited to accept reserve field artillery commissions with the assignment of attending summer camps as morale builders for the ROTC and reserve officer groups.

"Our friendship developed almost instantaneously and it soon included our families to the point that our daughters went to school together, both joined the same sorority and the Junior League, took part in each other's wedding and each became godmother of the other's children. It was this continuous close friendship that led Mr. Truman to ask me to give up the offer of the presidency of the First National Bank in St. Louis, Missouri, and come to Washington to help him after he became President.

"In this connection, I served as his Secretary of the Treasury for nearly seven years.

"In 1940 it was my pleasure to introduce to Senator Truman a very dear friend of mine from St. Louis, Stuart Symington, who at the time was president of Emerson Electric Company. . . . After Mr. Truman became President, he, upon my recommendation, invited Symington to come to Washington. Among other important assignments given him by President Truman was the honor of becoming the first Secretary of the Air Force of the newly formed Defense Department.

"So as you can see, there was a deep-rooted reason for the two of us to undertake the creation of a memorial for our good friend.

"My first conviction, as I expressed it to Senator Symington, was that President Truman would not want a pile of bricks and mortar commemorating the past, but would much prefer a memorial that would build for the future.

"It was with this thought in mind that I began the development of the plan for a Scholarship Foundation, education having been one of the continuing topics of discussion between President Truman and me through the years. . . ."

The foundation, which is funded and supervised by the government, annually awards four-year scholarships to fifty-three young students (one from each state, the District of Columbia and Puerto Rico, and the last from an island possession) to help prepare them for political careers.

Besides this topic, Mr. Snyder in our conversation skipped agilely over a number of others, including:

• *Henry Wallace,* who, I was surprised to hear, was still around as well as rolling in riches from a kind of hybrid corn he developed. I asked about Wallace's often quoted comment that Truman, as President, seemed to be going in different directions at once. Snyder shrewdly replied that the waffling effect might have been caused by Wallace's own stance, much as the horizon might look askew to someone on a sinking ship. In fact, he indicated that Wallace had come lately to feel that he *had* been on a sinking ship. ("He told me he'd listened to a lot of bad advice.") Turned conservative now, he regrets his Madison Square Garden speech and his party-splitting in 1948.

"I respect people's problems," Snyder added, suggesting that this attitude had enabled him to stay on good terms with Wallace, and also Eisenhower, without damage to his relations with Truman.

• *Eisenhower and Truman:* Ostensibly the two composed their differences at the funeral of Sam Rayburn, where they shook hands. But despite that gesture, and a couple of other polite exchanges, Ike, said Snyder, never forgave Truman for the remarks he made in the 1952 campaign, nor did Truman ever forgive *him* his failure to defend the reputation of General Marshall. Before leaving the subject, Snyder remarked that General MacArthur's resentment over Ike's being named Supreme Commander in Europe had sparked his later rebelliousness—a theory I hadn't heard before.

• *The Bomb:* I mentioned my talk with Truman about the Bomb, and Snyder said that Roosevelt also had been troubled by the thought that the new weapon might destroy the world but that Einstein had reassured him. Snyder himself had become aware of the Bomb while he was in charge of the Defense Plant Corporation. He had had to fund some of the ancillary nuclear operations and after one sniff of the Bomb itself had leaned over backward to learn no more.

• *Truman and Pendergast:* The former needed professional political backing, the latter a candidate of good repute; that was all there was to that.

• *Truman and poker:* Not being a good poker player himself, Snyder said, he couldn't really judge Truman's ability. The latter, he went on, enjoyed poker not from any great fondness for it as a game or from an itch to win, but because of the comradeship it offered and the chance to study people's characters.

• *Reunions:* There seemed to have been a lot of horseplay at Truman-Snyder-Vaughan-McKim get-togethers, I said. Could he give me an example? Well, said Snyder, lighting up a little, a favorite joke had been to test a recruit by telling him there was a dangerous animal pent up in a box, which he was ordered to open. Inside would be a chamber pot.

The telephone on the desk rang twice while we were talking. The second time clearly signaled the end of the interview, and I hastened to get in a final question: What was his considered opinion of Harry Truman as President?

"Truman," he said, "was one of the greatest humanitarians ever to hold the office. He was for the people."

On my way out, I thought that Mr. Snyder's brain still was ticking over nicely. I could understand Truman's reliance on him. I also would have been willing to bet that he was a better poker player than he professed to be.

XII

Retrospective

A GREAT HUMANITARIAN? WELL, MAYBE, BUT THAT HAS A BIG SOUND. At least, there's no doubt about Truman's being human. Although H. V. Kaltenborn went agley in reporting the 1948 election, he was not a distinguished radio commentator for nothing. He certainly was right in saying that "for the next four years we can all be human with Truman."

"Human" often is used pejoratively, as in "to err is human," which in 1948 the Republicans revised to read, "To err is Truman." By now the joke seems more compliment than jibe, since in these days of overgrown population, overgrown businesses, overgrown government, humanity—or better, humanness—is becoming an endangered quality.

Anyhow, Truman had it. And he went out of his way to treat others not as "bodies" or digits but as fellow human beings. He was happy to discuss the problems of government with anybody who seemed interested, traveled all over asking questions, helped people who needed help and told them to go to hell when he thought they needed that.

Take his manner of dealing with the music critic who lambasted one of Margaret's concerts. It is not hard to imagine how the most egregious of his successors would have handled that problem. On the evidence, Nixon would have avoided any confrontation with the offender; he'd have pulled strings, brought pressure to bear and tried to get the man fired from his job. Truman let loose his wrath in a handwritten, self-mailed letter, promising the recipient even closer personal contact if he so wished. The results were happy all around: Margaret was spared the humiliation she feared, her father enjoyed the catharsis and the critic sold the letter for a handsome sum.

Truman's humanness, I think, nourished the affability that so impressed Ambassador Stanley Woodward [1] and the charm that many others (including me) were surprised to find in him. It not only won him friends but frequently had an odd effect on them. Just as innocence is a suspenseful quality because of the difficulties plainly lying in wait for anyone who has it, so too was this humanness of Truman's. You could feel that it was going to get him in trouble, and you wanted to help. The most unlikely people felt this way about him, tough Irishmen like McKim and Connelly and Vaughan, who was so beset by troubles himself that you would not have expected him to have time for somebody else's.

The phenomenon is particularly evident in a couple of reminiscences of McKim's and Connelly's. Recalling the vice-presidential campaign of 1944, McKim says:

"I was supposedly in charge of the train, and I was also kind of in charge of Mr. Truman. I had to see that he got to bed on time, that he ate the proper food; and when he would go out in the crowds, I always walked to his left and immediate rear, the idea being that so many of these politicians have got the idea that they've got to slap the candidate on the back. Well, after a few of those during the day, you can knock a fellow out. And I got rather adept at knocking off those big hands in the air.

"Another thing: I usually wore a topcoat, and of course a vice-presidential candidate is not entitled to have Secret Service protection. I always carried my left hand in my pocket with the knuckles sticking out, like I had a gun there. And nobody knew whether or not I was a Secret Service man, but I was along for the protection of the candidate, to keep him from being hit. You get up in that Northwest country, some of those big lumberjacks, they've got hands like hams. Two or three of those and the candidate would be hors de combat."

Connelly's contribution is even stranger. The conversation he is recalling took place during one of the presidential vacations at Key West, Florida. Truman said he wanted to ask him something and added that he didn't want a snap answer.

"I said, 'Well, ask me. I don't know how to answer until I hear the question.'

"So he said, 'How would you like to be Postmaster General and chairman of the National Committee?'

"I said, 'The answer is no.'

[1] See Chapter V, p. 65.

"He said, 'I told you to think about it.'"

"I said, 'That's right, you did. I did think about it, and the answer is still no.'"

"He says, 'You know what you're turning down?'"

"I said, 'Yes.'"

"He said, 'Why? This isn't offered to many.'"

"I said, 'Yes, I know why.' I said, 'With you I belong at the rathole. So I'll stay to protect you at that rathole. I know the deal. That's why my answer is no.'"

"End of discussion."

Asked if he ever had any regrets, he answered:

"No, but I did know that there's where my value to him was, to protect him from the interlopers."

Humanness seems to have been built into Truman's character early in life. It was placed there mostly by the examples of his mother, father and grandparents, who embodied the values and characteristics of frontier days: honesty, hard work, courage, canniness, optimism. He was a walking reminder of an America long gone, buried under the detritus of years of new ways, new goals, but still giving off an occasional gleam that strikes us with nostalgia and evokes a sense of loss. He was the last President in whom it was possible to catch a glimpse of that far-off time. A little of it showed in Eisenhower, but it was overlaid by the military training that made him special; and his successors, of course, were born too late to have had any firsthand experience of it.

Truman was a citizen-soldier in the old tradition, ready to take up arms in emergencies and to drop them when things got better. And it was the affairs of citizens, of ordinary people, that preoccupied him. In fact, he looked upon the President as the single person in government who had been chosen to represent, not some limited interest or group, but the people in general. A kind of all-purpose speech I came across among his papers states the case:

"I am going to ask you to come to the White House this evening and sit with me on my side of the desk. All day I sit here facing people—all sorts of people—wanting something—all asking me to do something. But on my side of the desk I sit alone, conscious that with me in spirit are millions and millions of people without organization; without voice; without representation in the White House—except as I can give it to them.

"I am President of the WHOLE people. That is my job. It is easy to be President of part of the people. It is easy to be President of the part of the people who run the railroads. It is harder to be President of the people who must use the railroads. It is easy to be President of the part of the people who have meat to sell—hard to be President of those who have to buy it.

"I look upon these United States as a great Union—a Union of ALL the states; of ALL the people in it. My title is PRESIDENT of the United States—not one state—or a few—or a part—but of ALL of the States of the Union—of ALL the United States and ALL the people in them. . . ."

A few other characteristics of Truman's—besides his humanness, or as part of it—stand out in retrospect. In the first chapter of this book, for instance, there was a good deal of discussion of his retirement, of the ease and grace with which he made the transition from President to unemployed citizen of Independence, Missouri. As distinct from many of the retired, he was not losing identity, not drifting. By setting himself well-defined objectives and by keeping to home waters, among the landmarks of the past, he was able to steer a straight course.

In fact, I've never met anyone whose idea of his own identity was clearer than Truman's. There was nothing passive about this. He seemed to be as interested in ascertaining his exact position in space and time as the pilot of a ship or plane is in ascertaining his.

When he made up his mind to drive to Washington with Mrs. Truman in June 1953, he got out the maps, plotted the route and told me precisely how many miles it was from his front door to the door of the Senate garage. He added with some pride that his knowledge of maps probably was greater than that of any other President.

The same navigational bent was evident in his reading. Five or six daily papers, backed up by quantities of books, mostly biography and history, provided him with still another frame of reference. But he didn't much care for editorials or the theories of historians, he said. "I like to draw my own conclusions, if I can get the facts. I've always tried to get all the information I could on every job I ever had." And with a typical fillip, "So nobody could put anything over on me."

He also remarked that any President who didn't do his own reading and plenty of it was asking for trouble. The reference was to Eisenhower, who, he had been told, had his staff predigest each day's essential information and present it to him in headline form. How could anybody base sound judgments, sound decisions, on headlines? You had to have the facts.

Truman was known, of course, for the decisions he made while he was President. Once in talking about them he expressed an idea I found enlightening. It showed how they had been arrived at, and again the process seemed to be that of determining his position. If, he said, while sitting in the White House, he had thought of himself as plain Harry Truman deciding the fate of the world, he'd have been paralyzed. Instead, he had understood that the decisions hadn't been up to him; they had been up to the President of the United States, "whom I happened to be temporarily."

"That," he added, "may seem like a fine distinction, but I'm glad I made it; otherwise I might be suffering from the same kind of importance complex a few other Presidents came down with. . . ."

Fine or not, it's a distinction anyone unable to see himself in perspective would have had trouble making. It also is one that could prove helpful to others. If bottled and sold as a remedy, that fine distinction might do wonders for many a retired man of distinction, who can't quite believe he still isn't director of this or chairman of that. It might even help him be a more engaging human being. For the ability to know exactly, to the inch and minute, who one is and where one is seems to have a beneficial effect not only on one's course but on one's character. It promotes humanness.

A Kansas City taxi driver, who delivered me to the building where Truman then had his office, asked if I were going to see "Harry." When I said I was, he continued, "Well, you can say this about him. He never got the big head. They put on all the heat they had but he just grinned and beared it. . . ."

As the words suggested, modesty had been included in the Truman public image. But it was more noticeable in private. I remember the first time I heard him speak of General George Marshall. It surprised me that a President of the United States could entertain for anyone feelings as boyishly admiring as his were for Marshall. And, aware of his reputation as a cusser and poker player, I was not prepared for the courtliness he always showed his wife and other women, or for his considerate handling of people who sometimes seemed to make a point of imposing on him.

At lunch one time in the Pickwick Hotel, the autograph hounds and hand shakers were so aggressive he scarcely had a chance to eat. When I commented on the fact later, he laughed and said he tried to put himself in their place and think how he'd feel "if some supposed bigshot high-hatted me."

More than once that spring I was reminded of Kipling's lines about the man who could talk with crowds and keep his virtue "or walk with Kings —nor lose the common touch." They might have been written with Truman in mind. Indeed, of the few famous men with whom my work had brought me in contact, he was the only one who after a heady experience of power still appeared to be complete as a person.

It was his unpretentiousness that kept me from realizing half the time that he was talking *history*. Churchill, Stalin and de Gaulle to him were unusual men, but, on the other hand, so were some of the fellows he saw each day. And it was the same with the great figures of the past. In listening to him speak of Washington and Jefferson and the other fathers of our country, I'd sometimes get the feeling that he had known them personally and also that some of them must have been not unlike him. They too had been born navigators. At least, they'd done a pretty good job of charting the nation's course.

He was particularly taken with their view of the presidency, with the idea that, as he put it, "Anybody can be President, and, when he reaches the end of his term, he can go back to being anybody again. It's the job that counts, not the man."

That struck him as the essence of democracy, and, seen through his eyes, it did me, too. In fact, it must be about the highest compliment ever paid the average man. Even knowing it's true, it's hard to believe that any political system in its routine workings regularly hands some more or less ordinary citizen enough power to dazzle a dictator, then drops him back into the everyday world and expects him to carry on as though nothing much had happened.

Compared with his retirement, anybody else's is bound to seem a minor matter. Occasionally, when I manage to see my own in that perspective, I am thankful to Truman for having helped me do so, and the memory of how he accepted his brings back a thought that first occurred to me in 1953.

When I arrived in Independence, my attitude was not much different from the one he attributed to the tourists, who used to flock around his home.

"They all want to get a look at the striped mule of Missouri," he said.

By the time I left, the looks I'd gotten had made me think that the striped mule of Missouri would make almost as appropriate a national emblem as the eagle.

Postscript

IN WRITING ABOUT GOING TO WASHINGTON IN JUNE 1953 TO SEE TRUMAN in that setting, I mentioned a dinner in his honor at which Dean Acheson gave the main speech.

"Best tribute to T.," I jotted down in my notes, "to almost anybody I ever heard. Tried to get a copy but couldn't."

Well, in the fall of 1977, I did get a copy. It was in what's called the Post-Presidential File of the Truman Library.

Dean Acheson is gone now, but his son, David, a Washington lawyer, has given me permission to quote the speech. I do so gratefully, for it seems to me to be still, after twenty-five years, the best tribute to anybody I ever heard, and the best possible conclusion to this book:

"Mr. President, Mrs. Truman, Margaret: This large and happy official family of yours has selected its most indigent member to express a little of what is in their hearts at the reunion with you. I know very well what is in my heart, because I experienced it suddenly and vividly yesterday afternoon. I was walking along H Street after lunch when I heard a vigorous honking of an automobile horn. I knew, of course, that this was not directed at me, for, as you can readily understand, no sane citizen of Washington would willingly be seen talking with me on the street. However, in a few seconds Dave Stowe [1] appeared around the back of a bakery truck. I was only mildly surprised at this because I thought that, after all, the poor fellow had to get a bun some way. He pointed to a large, shiny limousine and said that a friend of mine wanted to speak with me. And there, framed in the window, was the President's beaming face. At that moment I knew how the Korean prisoners felt when the guards opened the stockade gates.

"Mr. President, we are all reliably informed that among the Mohammedans the faithful turn to the East when they pray. In Washington the

---

[1] An aide of President Truman's.

faithful turn to the West. And so your return is to us a very real answer to prayer.

"For this is a very different town from the one you left a little over five months ago. I shall not harrow you and Mrs. Truman with horror stories about what has occurred. It is illustration enough for you to think of the spectacle of Charlie Murphy [2] and me getting on a street car for the first time in years and not even knowing what the fare was.

"Washington has become a city of rumors and doubts. There is even a rumor that at the present time no one at all lives in the White House, and, so far, no one has ever been able to prove or disprove the rumor by any of the facts at hand.

"Similar reports come to us from overseas. Recently a friend of mine returned from London. He had arrived there on the same day that Messrs. Cohn and Schine [3] arrived, but he was innocent of any knowledge of this dire event. As Averell [4] will remember from his London experience, within a few feet of the Embassy is the Connaught Hotel, with its spacious and pleasant bar, where employees of the Embassy were accustomed to fortify themselves with a gentle martini before facing the rigors of the London subway on their way home. My friend went there as the most likely spot to gather the current gossip. He found it completely deserted. A paralyzed pall had come over the Embassy, such as we are informed occurs at night in the jungle when the tiger is abroad. No one in the Embassy would run the risk of being seen partaking of alcoholic beverages. A few of the more cautious souls thought it unwise even to speak to their wives because they had misplaced their marriage certificates and could not prove the relationship. The old bartender was in the bar alone, sadly polishing the glasses. My friend said, 'George, what goes on? Where is everybody?' At which the bartender replied, 'Don't you know, sir? It is the Mau Mau. Run for your life.'

"We are particularly happy and heartened that you have brought Mrs. Truman and Margaret with you. You will recall that in certain tense and dangerous places in the world we frequently thought to strengthen the morale of the local population by having our officers go to their posts accompanied by their wives and families. So, when we see you accompanied by Mrs. Truman and Margaret, we all say to one another with new spirit, 'You see, it can't be as bad as it seems.'

"The other day I was discussing some of the local phenomena with the

---

[2] A legal adviser to President Truman.

[3] Investigators for Senator Joseph McCarthy of Wisconsin.

[4] Among the many jobs William Averell Harriman undertook for Truman was that of Ambassador to Great Britain (April–October 1946).

former legal adviser of the Department of State, the Honorable Butch Fisher. He was commenting on—what shall we call it?—the apparent lack of resolution on the part of some of the representatives of the executive branch in dealing with senatorial committees. He said that his first thought was that we should congratulate ourselves that we were men of stouter fiber. He then thought of a recent episode, where a Cabinet officer appearing to defend a current administration measure, said, in answer to questions, that he was neither for it nor against it. Fisher then observed that perhaps the difference between the present situation and ours was not so much in superior virtue on our part but in our knowledge that there were no terrors or dangers upon the Hill which would remotely approximate the lethal encounter which would await us at the White House if we returned to it from any such performance as that I have mentioned.

"Perhaps that is another way of saying that we had and knew that we had leadership; that it is leadership which makes all things possible.

"The other day I was asked by a group of undergraduates at Yale to explain to them a matter upon which they had received little or no enlightenment from our American press, which was once referred to, as I recall it, by a distinguished gentleman as a one-party press. What was it, they asked, about the President of the United States who held office until noon on January 20, 1953, which inspired such devoted loyalty on the part of all who worked with him? This was a task so easy and pleasant that even in my present relaxed—not to say lazy—condition I happily and eagerly responded to it.

"I shall not embarrass you by the full account, which was far too long for this occasion. One thought, I think, is appropriate here. Loyalty, I said to the young men, is not something which is understood solely by considering those who give it. It requires an understanding of him who inspires it. The finest loyalty is not apt to be inspired by a man unless he inspires both respect and affection. Respect comes for many reasons. It is enough here to say that it springs from the fundamental purposes of a man's life and from his methods of achieving them, his manner of conducting himself in his relations with others.

"President Truman's fundamental purpose and burning passion has been to serve his country and his fellow citizens. This devoted love of the United States has been the only rival which Mrs. Truman has had. It has never been obscured or deflected by thought of himself, by personal ambition, or desire for position. What he has wanted for the United States is what every decent citizen has wanted for his own family, his own neighbors, his own community and country. It has not been to have it big or rich or powerful for these ends themselves. It has not been to use its power to dictate either to its own people or to other people. His ambition has not been for a country where the powerful grow more powerful, the rich grow richer, and the poor grow poorer.

"He has sought in every way to give full scope for ability, energy and initiative to create abundance beyond anything we have thought possible. But he has sought to do more. He has sought to make a kind and compassionate country whose institutions would truly reflect, both at home and abroad, the kind and compassionate nature of its people. He has sought to keep opportunity open to all and to mold political and economic life so that the weak and unfortunate are not trampled and forgotten, and so that all who honestly strive to do the best they can may fairly share in the abundance which this country creates. These are purposes which excite the respect and enthusiasm of all who have been fortunate enough to work with him.

"But, as I said a moment ago, methods are quite as important as purposes. And here we all know that the President has insisted that all the cards should be on the table. He has hated and abhorred intrigue and double-dealing. He has not tolerated yes men, but has insisted that all of us should state our opinions forthrightly and honestly. He has not been afraid of differences of opinion. Time and time again they have been brought to him, and time and time again he has done the hardest of all things— faced issues and made decisions. And all of us have known that the decisions were conscientiously and bravely made and to us these decisions were law.

"These are qualities enough to bring respect and to engender affection. But there has been more.

"The greatest of all commanders never ask more of their troops than they are willing to give themselves. They share the dangers with their men, the bitterness of defeat, the sweat and struggle of the battle. The President has never asked any of us to do what he would not do. When the time came to fight, he threw everything into it, himself included. And what we all knew was that, however hot the fire was in front, there would never be a shot in the back. Quite the contrary! He stood by us through thick and thin, always eager to attribute successes to us and to accept for himself the full responsibility for failure. Not one of us has had a trouble in our public or private lives that he has not been quick to know of and quick to ease.

"It is not strange, Mr. President, that you have had, and have, the devotion and loyalty of this official family of yours here tonight and of millions of others who have not been privileged to work so closely with you.

"It is for reasons such as these that this visit of yours brings us such happiness. These visits of yours must be regular affairs, for we all badly need the refreshment and inspiration that they bring to us.

"To you, Mr. President, and to your enduring health and happiness, we join in a final toast."

Index